Nick Nairn's Top 100 Chicken Recipes

To Daisy Skye Nairn

# nick nairn's top 100
# CHICKEN
## recipes

Quick and easy dishes for every occasion

BBC
BOOKS

# Contents

# Introduction

## Chicken tonight?

My reason for writing this book is not just to illustrate the speed and convenience of cooking with chicken but also to celebrate its versatility. Chicken can provide a huge range of meal solutions, from a perfectly roasted bird served, simply, with its own gravy, to a bewildering variety of uses in soups, sautées, stir-fries and casseroles.

'Poultry is for the cook what canvas is to the painter' – so said the gastronome Brillat-Savarin. And it's true. Chicken is a great vehicle for all flavours from Mediterranean and Indian to Southeast Asian and Caribbean.

Today, chicken is more popular than ever, with the biggest seller being packs of breast fillets. Easy to prepare and quick to cook, they are a popular choice and people often combine them with jar sauces for a quick and tasty meal. But what about the rest of the bird? The high demand for breast fillets means that thighs, drumsticks, wings and livers are in plentiful supply, making them relatively low-priced and affordable. And don't think cheaper means second best – for flavour I'd choose thighs over breasts any time, and you can't beat pan-fried chicken livers for speed and great flavour.

## Choosing your chicken

A few basic factors determine the quality of the chicken you buy. In the UK, a British flag on the packaging generally indicates a superior bird, and if a chicken is a specified breed this is also a good indication of quality. Some supermarkets carry at least one quality, breed-specific bird, but a good poultry dealer will be able to advise you of the different varieties available in your area.

At the top of the quality range are organic free-range chickens. These birds are reared for at least 80–90 days, and are expensive as a result. They are free to roam and are fed on a diet of organic grain and water. These really are the Rolls-Royces of the chook world, and if you're looking for real concentrated chicken flavour and luscious, succulent flesh you won't be disappointed. Expensive, but for me worth every last penny.

Next we have free-range. Unfortunately, due to United Kingdom labelling nonsense, not every free-range chicken is as 'free' as the next one, so look for the terms 'traditional free-range' and 'total freedom free-range'. These birds have varying access to outdoors, are fed a mix of grain and pellets and are reared for 60–80 days. They offer excellent eating quality at a premium price. Look out for corn- or maize-fed chickens too – you'll recognize them by their yellow-hued flesh. Their corn-rich diet encourages a better flavour, but be aware that they can be intensively reared as well as free-range.

The good news for those on a tighter budget is that British legislation is improving the life of the battery chicken. For the past couple of decades price was the determining criterion for selling chicken – reduced price deals, buy one get one free – which meant that price was also the defining criterion for producing it. Hence, at its worst, a battery bird could be a sorry apology for a chicken – limp, tasteless and watery with a grainy texture. In recent years, minimum standards have been set for the welfare of chickens, and they appear to be having an effect without too much financial pressure on producers. Although the birds are far from running wild, rules governing the density at which they are kept mean they are able to move around. In addition, most producers have opted to follow the guidelines restricting the non-medicinal use of antibiotics and, more pertinently, growth-inducing hormones. If you buy a chicken labelled 'produced in Britain' you can be reassured that strict regulations have been followed from hatching to slaughter. However, the life of a battery chicken is short – usually just 42 days – which means it will never come close to an organic or free-range bird for flavour. It would never be my choice for roast chicken; in a curry perhaps, it would be a different matter.

But what about really cheap chickens? These are usually imported, most notably from Thailand where birds are intensively reared without any of the regulations or health and safety laws required in the United Kingdom. I would never buy imports, with the exception of premium French birds, but you may well be consuming them unintentionally. Watch out for chicken labelled 'packaged in Britain' – this doesn't mean it's British poultry, just that it is wrapped in Britain.

## How to use this book

The aim of this book is to inspire you to move on from dishes knocked up from a pack of breast fillets and a jar of stir-in sauce. Whatever cut you wish to cook, there's a recipe for it. Perhaps you only ever cook breasts or a whole roast bird, and are unsure of the best way to use thighs – well, here you'll find the cooking methods

## Jointing a chicken

The most important thing to remember when jointing a chicken is that at no point do you have to cut through bone. To remove the legs (1), slash through the skin between the leg and the body. Prize it away from the carcass until it pops out of its socket. Place the chicken on its side and use a sharp knife to cut between the thigh and the carcass to release the leg. To remove the wings (2), cut between the wing joint and the body. To remove the breasts (3), cut down from the top using the breastbone as a guide. Change the angle of the knife when you reach the wishbone and continue cutting until you meet the carcass. Gently score between the bird and the breast until it comes away.

and techniques to help you on your way to kitchen success. Each recipe has been categorized, illustrating how easy it is to make and whether it's best as a snack, an informal supper or an impressive dinner-party dish. For me, this book is a collection of versatile recipe ideas, all simple and easy to follow. I hope it will be a regular reference book in your kitchen.

## Whole chickens

A whole roast chicken is one of life's great pleasures – no frills no fuss, but immensely satisfying with its crisp skin and aromatic juices. The recipe for My Perfect Roast Chicken Dinner (see page 112) is exactly what it says: perfect. With the addition of lemons, garlic and parsley (see page 113), roast chicken is quite possibly the best meal in the world. There are variations on the theme, like putting stuffing in the cavity or between the skin and breast, that produce a myriad flavours and textures, but the basic technique remains the same.

For the best results remove your bird from the fridge a good 30 minutes before cooking to allow it to come to room temperature; and always follow the cardinal rule of resting it for 10–15 minutes after roasting and before carving. This allows the juices that have welled up near the skin to seep back into the flesh as the meat relaxes, making it more succulent. If you want plump and juicy breasts, turn the chicken upside down whilst it's relaxing.

There are other options for cooking a whole chicken – my current favourite is barbecuing. You need a kettle-style barbecue that will cook with indirect heat, but you have to try this method to believe the results – the crisp skin is so shiny it looks like it's been varnished

1

2

3

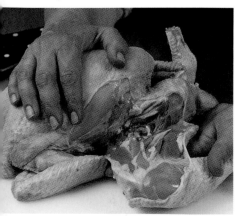

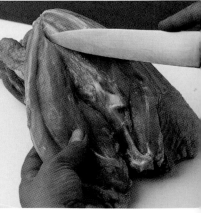

and the meat is infused with great smoky flavours.

One of the most satisfying things is to buy a whole chicken and joint it. For the price of a couple of breast fillets you can just about buy a whole bird – and, as I describe below, use everything but the 'cheep'. Once you've done this, don't forget the carcass, which is perfect for making Light Chicken Stock (see page 14).

## Different cuts of chicken

Breast fillets are the ideal size for single portions, are low in fat (when the skin is removed) and there is no wastage at all. With their tender white meat, they should be treated like steak and cooked quickly over a high heat – but take care not to overcook them. They are great for pan-frying (see my Peppered Chicken with Whisky Sauce on page 72) and also for griddling, barbecuing and steaming. Or, cut into thin escalopes or cubed, they are the perfect choice for kebabs and speedy stir-fries. Popular and easy breast fillets may be, but they're also the most expensive way to buy chicken.

Thighs are tougher than other cuts and a little on the fatty side. However, this means they are packed full of flavour, economical and ideal for slow cooking in casseroles. My favourite way to cook thighs is over a low heat in a frying pan. It takes a little time, but the result is delicious crispy skin, reminiscent of crackling, and succulent, well-flavoured flesh – perfect in my Warm Salad of Crispy Chicken Thighs (see page 36).

Drumsticks are the lower part of the legs and, again, are ideal for casseroles. They are also great for roasting or throwing on the barbecue. If you're doing the latter I'd recommend poaching them for

**Jointing a chicken continued**

To separate the drumsticks and thighs (4), place the leg on its side with the drumstick pointing up. Push the drumstick back until the joint pops out, then cut. To bone the thigh (5), place it skin side down and make an incision either side of the bone. Rotate and repeat until the bone comes free. Slide the knife underneath and cut the bone free at one end. Hold the thigh by the bone and scrape the flesh free. Cut around the base of the bone until it comes free. Repeat with the drumstick. The drumstick has two bones, so take care to slide the knife below them both. You will be left with two drumsticks, two wings, two livers, two thighs, two breasts and a carcass (6).

4

5

6

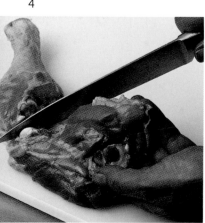

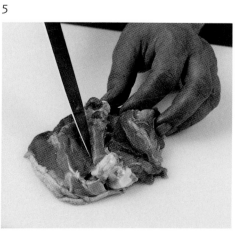

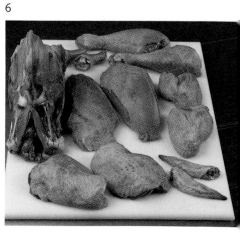

ten minutes first, to avoid drumsticks that are cooked on the outside but jelly-like in the middle. I like to pile on the robust flavours – as in my Paprika and Red Pepper Chicken (see page 87) – and drumsticks take extremely well to the eastern flavours of China, Thailand and my own personal favourite: India. Eating with your fingertips is the most underrated sensuous eating experience, and drumsticks simply weren't made for cutlery!

Wings also make great finger food, perfect for parties and barbecues. They have dark-meat-like flesh and, because they are small, are pretty inexpensive cuts that not only offer value for money but are great for nibbling on. Like drumsticks, wings are great for big flavours and really need a marinade or coating to make them special. My Spicy Barbecued Chicken Wings (see page 111) are always a sure-fire party hit.

Livers are ludicrously cheap and really are life's last affordable luxury. When I was growing up I was always highly suspicious of any kind of offal, none more so than chicken livers. But when I finally tasted them – a revelation! Since then I've been a fan of their versatility, from pink and squidgy in a warm salad to silky smooth in a pâté. One piece of advice though. Freezing turns livers into a dull mushy pap that's OK for pâté but nothing else, so, for any other recipe buy fresh, not frozen, ones.

## Food poisoning

Chicken does pose a risk of salmonella poisoning, but making sure the meat is thoroughly cooked through will kill any bacteria in the flesh. Always wash your hands and equipment after handling a raw bird and ensure that cooked chicken is kept well away from any equipment used for its raw preparation as it can easily be recontaminated. Finally, a frozen chicken must be thoroughly defrosted before cooking as cold pockets will allow bacteria to breed by preventing the meat reaching the required temperature.

## Wines to drink with chicken

Just as there are endless flavour combinations for cooking chicken, there's no limit to the variety of wines to match. There are no hard or fast rules, but these combinations work for me.

For classic roast chicken, it has to be a large glass of chilled classic, oaked Chardonnay. Its smooth buttery aroma should match the succulence and subtlety of the meat. As a rule of thumb, I usually spend at least as much on the wine as on the bird. Other whites that would work here include Pinot Gris from the Alsace, Viognier from anywhere and a dry Semillon with a few years of age from Australia. For red-wine lovers, I'd suggest low-tannin, smooth reds like Cru Beaujolais, or perhaps a decent red Burgundy. Smooth Grenache-based reds, from south Australia or southern France and Spain, are also a good bet.

Similar wines can work with pasta- and rice-based dishes, but I'd recommend experimenting with a ripe rosé – a personal favourite is Rioja Rosado. For gutsier one-pan rice dishes like Paella (see page 65) and Jambalaya (see page 57) that call for a little more acidity, try a chablis or a ripe Sauvignon Blanc from Australia or California.

There are a number of eastern dishes in the book and if a recipe includes citrus fruits, sweet marinades or oriental herbs, reach for the much-maligned Riesling grape. The refreshing, clean taste of a top German Riesling provides the perfect contrast to a spicy, sticky chicken dish such as Hot, Sweet and Sour Chicken (see page 110).

Last but not least, on to casseroles. The recipes in this section are generally fairly gutsy and robust, so start to explore reds. Coq au Vin (see page 128) originated in a part of France that's not a million miles away from the district of Champagne, so the local wine used in the dish was probably a lightish red. For authenticity, a Beaujolais, Macon Rouge or similar is the one to go for.

## Cook's notes

I'm convinced many of the best ideas and combinations in cooking often come about by accident rather than design. I also believe you learn something every time you cook, and that the difference between professional chefs and home cooks is simply that the professionals have had a tad more practice. The more experience you have in the kitchen, the easier it all becomes – you learn that a roasting tin isn't just for roasting; you can cook with it on the hob or use it to contain batter. If you have a thermometer and a wok you have a deep-fat fryer. Over time you'll decide what equipment is essential to you – I can't work without good-quality knives and always insist on heavy-based, stainless steel cookware.

Fresh chicken stock is essential in some of the recipes here, but a good-quality stock cube is fine for others. Butter should be unsalted unless otherwise stated. For seasoning, I use Maldon sea salt for its flavour and pepper is always black and freshly ground.

# 1 Cooking Perfect Chicken

| Quick and easy |
| --- |
| Preparation time<br>20–30 minutes |
| Serves 6 |

4 x chicken joints (breasts, thighs, drumsticks or wings)

freshly ground sea salt and freshly ground black pepper

olive oil

a little butter

a squeeze of fresh lemon juice

One of the greatest attractions of chicken is its versatility. When it comes to cooking it, however, it is important to match the correct cooking technique to each individual cut in order to achieve the best results. These are my favourite techniques for cooking each cut, along with a few simple tips for obtaining perfect results, every time. Whichever method you choose, it is vital that you let the chicken rest for 5–10 minutes before serving.

**The perfect chicken breast** Even if you are worried about eating chicken skin for health reasons, I recommend cooking the breast with the skin on and removing it afterwards. The meat will be moist, with bags of flavour and a great colour. Season the breast all over with salt and pepper. Heat a heavy frying pan until medium hot, then add a teaspoon of olive oil and a small knob of butter. Once the butter has melted into the oil and is starting to foam, add the breast, skin-side down. Brown for about 5 minutes, without moving it, then flip it over, turn down the heat and continue to cook for another 5–10 minutes (depending on the thickness). I like to finish the breast off by placing the frying pan in a hot oven (200°C/400°F/Gas Mark 6) for 10–15 minutes – that way the heat penetrates all around the chicken and the skin crisps up really well. Insert a small sharp knife into the thickest part of the flesh. If the juices run clear, the chicken is cooked. Squeeze a dash of lemon juice over the breast, then transfer to a warm plate, cover and rest for 5 minutes before serving.

**The perfect chicken thigh** There are only two ways to cook chicken thighs – braising or slow-roasting. As thigh meat is completely different to breast meat – slightly tougher and with a strong flavour – it needs long, slow cooking to tenderize it and bring out the full flavour. Braising means the meat is browned, then cooked slowly in a liquid or sauce, as in Braised Chicken with Leeks, Bacon and Caramelized Onions on page 131. To slow-roast, heat a medium-sized non-stick frying pan over a medium-to-low heat. Season the thighs well, then place them in the pan, skin-side down (they should fit snugly in the pan). Now cook the chicken without moving it, until the skin is nice and crispy. This will take about 30 minutes. It should slowly sizzle, so keep an eye on the pan and turn down the heat if it's sizzling too much. Once the thighs are well browned, turn them over and cook for another 2–3 minutes. Add a squeeze of lemon juice and shake the pan to make sure it's evenly distributed. Cook for another 3 minutes, then remove to a warm place to rest for 5 minutes.

**The perfect chicken drumstick** There is nothing worse than a flabby, under-cooked, chewy drumstick. They definitely need a longer cooking time than you would imagine and finishing them in the oven after browning in a frying pan crisps the skin and colours them all over. Preheat the oven to 200°F/400°F/Gas Mark 6. Season the drumsticks all over with salt and pepper. Brown the drumsticks as for the breasts, for about 3–5 minutes, without moving them, then flip them over, turn down the heat and finish in the oven until well cooked, brown and crispy – about 20–25 minutes depending on their size.

**The perfect chicken wing** I like to cook these on a kettle barbecue with the lid down. Season the wings well and baste with a marinade or basting sauce. Cook them for 20 minutes or so, basting intermittently. They will be succulent and sticky when cooked, and not covered in charcoal.

# 2  Quick Tomato Sauce

| Prepare in advance |
| --- |
| Preparation time 50 minutes |
| Makes 200 g (7 oz) |

**4 tablespoons olive oil**

**1 garlic clove, crushed**

**400 g can chopped tomatoes**

**2 tablespoons fresh basil leaves, torn**

**freshly ground sea salt and freshly ground black pepper**

The secret of this recipe is the cooking time – for a really thick and tasty sauce a good 30–45 minutes is essential. Make a large batch, which can be stored for up to 3 weeks in an airtight jar in the fridge. It's an extremely versatile sauce – it can be used as a pizza topping, as a last-minute addition to risotto or as a tasty pasta sauce. It's good both hot or cold. This quantity would cover four 25 cm/10 inch pizzas or serve four people with pasta.

**1** Heat the olive oil in a wide frying pan and add the garlic. Cook until the garlic is soft but not brown (when it will taste bitter) – about 1–2 minutes.

**2** Then add the chopped tomatoes, bring up to the boil and boil fast, stirring most of the time to stop the tomatoes sticking. Cook for 30–45 minutes until nice and thick. Stir in the basil and season well. Use as you like!

**NB** This is a quick sauce – hence the need for a wide pan to allow maximum evaporation. If you don't like the sauce too thick, just add a little water to thin it down. For a wickedly creamy version, stir in some milk at the end.

# 3 Light Chicken Stock

| Prepare in advance |
| --- |
| Preparation time 4 hours |
| Makes 1.3 litres (2¼ pints) |

**3 chicken carcasses, skin and fat removed**

**1 large carrot, quartered**

**1 leek, washed and quartered**

**2 celery sticks, halved lengthways**

**1 onion with skin left on, quartered**

**1 small head of garlic, halved across its equator**

**6 black peppercorns**

**1 bay leaf**

**a sprig of fresh thyme**

**a few fresh parsley or tarragon stalks**

Making stock can be a lengthy process, so it's best to tackle it when you have some spare time. I usually make the biggest possible batch by multiplying the ingredients to fill my largest stockpot. Then I put the stock into clearly labelled 600 ml (1 pint) tubs and freeze it for future use. Not only is it easier to make it in big batches but the stock will have a better flavour. In summer it's best to freeze stock immediately but in winter it will keep for up to 48 hours in the fridge. A good, rich chicken stock should have a slightly jellied consistency when cold.

Back in the old days, big hotels made rich chicken stock using whole chickens. This produced a deep, rich stock and the bonus of cooked chicken ready for room-service sandwiches – a fantastic if somewhat extravagant way to make stock. If you need a poached chicken, say for Coronation Chicken (see page 45), replace the three carcasses in this recipe with one medium chicken and follow the method below. Cutting the head of garlic across its 'equator' gives just the sweet garlic flavours and not the harsh garlic oil.

**1** Place the carcasses in a pan large enough for the bones to fill it only halfway. Just cover them with about 2.5 litres (4½ pints) cold water (too much water will dilute the flavour of the stock) and bring to the boil. Once boiling, reduce the heat immediately to a simmer and then, using a large spoon or ladle, skim off the fat and any scum from the surface. Add the rest of the ingredients, all of which should lie on top of the carcasses. Adjust the heat to a very slow simmer and skim once more.

**2** The simmering stock will now rise and fall through the vegetables, which act as a filter, absorbing all of the gunk from the liquid and leaving it crystal-clear. Leave it to simmer like this for 2–3 hours, tasting regularly. You should eventually notice the point at which the flavour stops improving. This means it's ready.

**3** Remove the pan from the heat and empty the stock into a colander set over a bowl. Now pass the stock through a fine sieve into a tall container or 2.5 litre (4½ pint) jug. Cover it and allow it to cool by placing it in a sink of cold water.

**4** When it's cool, place it in the fridge overnight. Skim off any fat that settles on top and spoon out the jellied stock into tubs. Freeze until ready to use.

# 4 Red Wine and Shallot Gravy

Stocks and sauces

| Prepare in advance |
| --- |
| Preparation time 25 minutes, plus soaking time |
| Makes about 300 ml (½ pint) |

**5 shallots, finely sliced**

**a sprig of fresh thyme**

**300 ml (½ pint) robust red wine (preferably Cabernet Sauvignon)**

**2 teaspoons fruit vinegar (e.g. raspberry or mixed fruit)**

**300 ml (½ pint) Light Chicken Stock (see opposite)**

**½ teaspoon redcurrant jelly**

**arrowroot, to thicken**

This is a really dark, rich and mellow gravy to make for special occasions. It keeps in the fridge (for around 4 days) or can be frozen, then added to the pan juices to deglaze a pan after cooking chicken pieces or roasting a chicken.

**1** Place the shallots and thyme in a stainless steel or glass bowl and cover with the wine and fruit vinegar. Cover and leave overnight in the refrigerator to infuse.

**2** The following day, pour the infusion into a thick-bottomed stainless steel pan and add the stock and redcurrant jelly. Place over a medium heat and bring gently to a slow simmer. Skim the surface to remove any scum as it forms and remove the thyme after about 10 minutes. Continue to reduce until the liquid is reduced by half – to about 300 ml (½ pint).

**3** When reduced, strain the sauce through a double layer of muslin into a bowl or jug. Use this as a sauce in its own right, thickened with a little slaked arrowroot, or add it to the pan juices after browning or roasting chicken, scraping up any sticky sediment, for a super-rich gravy.

# 5  White Sauce and Variations

| Prepare in advance |
| --- |
| Preparation time 20 minutes |
| Makes 600 ml (1 pint) |

50 g (2 oz) butter

25 g (1 oz) plain flour

600 ml (1 pint) whole milk

freshly ground sea salt and
freshly ground black pepper

Béchamel or white sauce is considered by many people to be an old-fashioned, lumpy, stodgy sauce, more associated with school canteens than gastronomy. I, however, am a fan of a well-made white sauce. The secret of success lies in properly cooking the sauce – and using more butter than flour in the roux makes this easy. Not only does it cook the flour properly but it makes it easier to whisk in the milk and keep the dreaded lumps at bay. It then needs another 10 minutes simmering to cook out the floury flavour.

There are two weapons in the battle against lumps in sauce: the electric hand whisk and the sieve. Forcing a lumpy sauce through the sieve into a clean pan and then giving it a good thrash with the electric whisk will restore most lumpy disasters to silky smooth sauces.

White sauce is a great base to which to add flavours – see below for ideas.

**1** Melt the butter in a small, heavy pan. Add the flour and, using a wooden spoon, stir over the heat for a minute or so until the mixture floods over the base of the pan and boils slowly – a bit like lava! Cook very slowly like this for at least 5 minutes, watching that it doesn't colour.

**2** Take the pan off the heat and, using a wire whisk, whisk in the milk all in one go. Make sure it is well blended.

**3** Return to the heat and slowly bring to the boil, whisking all the time. Turn down the heat and simmer very gently for 10 minutes, stirring occasionally to prevent a skin forming. Season to taste. This sauce can be cooled, covered and kept in the fridge and reheated (you may need to add a little more milk) when needed.

**Variations**

Add 100 g (4 oz) strong grated Cheddar or Gruyère cheese and a little Parmesan if you like. A touch of Dijon mustard will lift it!

Add 2–3 tablespoons wholegrain or Dijon mustard, depending on taste, for a mustard sauce.

Add 4 tablespoons chopped fresh herbs.

Add 6 tablespoons chopped blanched spinach and a little freshly grated nutmeg.

Add 30 g canned anchovies, drained and chopped.

# 6 Quick White Wine and Cream Sauce

| Quick and easy |
| --- |
| Preparation time 15 minutes |
| Serves 4 (about 300 ml/½ pint) |

15 g (½ oz) butter

2 shallots, sliced

4 button mushrooms, finely sliced

1 bay leaf

3 sprigs of fresh tarragon, leaves picked and chopped (retain stalks)

300 ml (½ pint) white wine

300 ml (½ pint) Light Chicken Stock (see page 14)

300 ml (½ pint) double cream

freshly ground sea salt and freshly ground black pepper

freshly squeezed lemon juice

This is the perfect luxurious sauce for when you are in a hurry and want to impress. It'll get a bit steamy in the kitchen as you reduce everything – but it's the reduction that really makes this sauce, by concentrating all the flavours. You could make it with a bit of stock cube and water as long as you finish it with some lemon juice and maybe some chopped fresh herbs, such as tarragon or chervil.

**1** Melt the butter in a pan over a low to medium heat and then sweat the shallots and mushrooms until they are soft. Add the bay leaf and tarragon stalks before increasing the heat to full and adding the wine. Bring to the boil and boil fast until it's nearly all gone.

**2** Now add the stock and reduce it by three-quarters.

**3** Then pour in the cream. Bring it to the boil, boil for a couple of minutes and then pour the contents of the pan through a fine sieve, forcing it through with the bottom of a ladle into a small, clean pan. Taste and season with salt and pepper, add the chopped tarragon leaves and a few drops of lemon juice to taste. Reheat to serve.

# 7 Béarnaise Sauce

| Smart entertaining |
|---|
| Preparation time 15 minutes |
| Serves 4 |

**2 shallots, very finely chopped**

**2 tablespoons white wine vinegar**

**1 tablespoon chopped fresh tarragon**

**2 egg yolks**

**juice of ¼ lemon**

**225 g (8 oz) Clarified Butter (see below), melted and cooled**

**a pinch of salt**

**a pinch of cayenne pepper**

This is an all-time classic and goes so well with chicken – especially chicken coated in breadcrumbs and fried. It is rich and buttery with a hint of tarragon. It is relatively easy to make – just watch that the water under the bowl doesn't get too hot and scramble the eggs.

Béarnaise should be regarded as a special-occasion sauce, partly as it requires a bit of effort with the whisk and partly as the heavenly combination of egg yolks, butter and lemon produces a sauce which is on the sinful side of healthy.

**1** Place the shallots, vinegar and tarragon in a small heavy-based pan. Bring to the boil and reduce by half. Strain the liquid through a fine sieve or muslin and reserve.

**2** Put the reserved liquid, egg yolks, 2 tablespoons water and the lemon juice into a heatproof bowl. Set over a pan of warm, but not boiling, water and using a fine wire whisk, whisk the mixture until it starts to thicken and the whisk leaves a visible trace in the mixture. This is hard work and will take about 5 minutes, but think of it as exercise! Remove the bowl from the heat and keep warm.

**3** Next, take the melted butter and, whisking continuously, pour a steady stream of butter into the cooked egg mixture. The butter must be poured at a slow, steady speed so that your whisking can absorb it into the egg mix, taking care not to let puddles form. (If it gets too thick, add a tablespoon or two of hot water.)

**4** When all of the butter has been incorporated into the egg mixture, add salt and cayenne pepper to taste. It may require another squeeze of lemon juice. Keep the mixture warm (about body temperature) until required, but be warned – if the mixture is overheated or allowed to cool, the sauce will separate. If this happens, it can easily be rescued by whisking the oily mess into a couple of fresh egg yolks and 3 tablespoons hot water.

## Clarified Butter
Clarified butter is obtained by heating unsalted butter gently until the fat separates from the whey. Simmer the butter, removing any scum that forms on the surface, until a clear fat layer is formed with a milky liquid below. Strain the clear layer through muslin carefully, leaving the milky whey behind in the pan, and refrigerate. It will keep for ages – just remember to cover it or keep it in a screw-top jar.

# 8 Barbecue Sauce

| |
|---|
| Prepare in advance |
| Preparation time 5 minutes |
| Makes about 225 ml (8 fl oz) |

**2 garlic cloves, crushed**

**1 teaspoon chopped fresh thyme**

**2 teaspoons sweet paprika**

**6 tablespoons tomato ketchup**

**4 tablespoons clear mild honey**

**juice and finely grated rind of 1 orange**

**2 tablespoons balsamic vinegar (or try sherry vinegar)**

**6 tablespoons light soy sauce**

**a dash of Tabasco sauce (I like the jalapeño one)**

**freshly ground sea salt and freshly ground black pepper**

**3 tablespoons chopped fresh coriander (optional)**

Everybody's got his or her favourite barbecue-sauce recipe and here's mine. I like to brush it over chicken joints or pieces when they are almost cooked. That way the sauce sticks to the chicken and glazes it without charring and burning before the chicken is cooked. Or serve it separately. I play around with these quantities quite a lot depending whether I want the sauce sweeter or punchier – feel free to adapt! If stored in an air-tight jar, this sauce will keep for up to 2 weeks in the fridge.

1 Smash the garlic and thyme together with the end of a rolling pin (or in a pestle and mortar).

2 Add to a pan with all the remaining ingredients, except the coriander, and slowly bring to the boil. Simmer for a few minutes until thickened. Then stir in the coriander, if using, and it's ready for you to use.

# 9 Sauce Vierge

| Informal supper |
| --- |
| Preparation time 15 minutes |
| Serves 4 |

125 ml (4 fl oz) olive oil

2 shallots, finely chopped or sliced

1 garlic clove, lightly crushed but left whole

4 ripe plum tomatoes, roughly chopped

2 tablespoons roughly chopped fresh basil

juice of ½ lemon

freshly ground sea salt and freshly ground black pepper

The posh name for virgin olive oil sauce, sauce vierge is essentially good-quality olive oil infused with Mediterranean flavours. I've tried many variations, but keep coming back to this recipe for its simple harmony of flavours. As with all simple recipes, the quality of the raw ingredients is important; here that means good-quality oil and ripe tomatoes. My current favourites are the small vine tomatoes or cherry plum tomatoes (*pomodorini*). In the restaurant we use fat plum tomatoes, which we skin and seed before dicing the flesh – a fiddly process that is more rewarding visually than to the taste buds. For home cooks, I recommend the more rustic approach of leaving the skin on and seeds in. Olive oil contains unsaturated fatty acids, which means that this sauce is healthier than ones made with butter – but, sadly, it's still fattening if you overindulge.

**1** Place the olive oil, shallots and garlic in a small pan. Warm through over a gentle heat until the sauce is hot, but not boiling – you want to soften the shallots, not colour them. Remove from the heat after 10 minutes and set aside. This can be made several days in advance and kept in the fridge.

**2** When ready to serve, lift out the garlic clove, stir in the tomatoes, basil and lemon juice, return to the heat to warm through and season to taste with salt and pepper.

# 10 Chicken Broth

| Informal supper |
| --- |
| Preparation time 45 minutes |
| Serves 4 |

1.2 litres (2 pints) Light Chicken Stock (see page 14)

40 g (1½ oz) long-grain rice

2 tablespoons diced carrot

2 tablespoons diced celery

2 tablespoons diced onion

2 tablespoons diced leek (white and green parts)

freshly ground sea salt and freshly ground black pepper

a squeeze of lemon juice

100 g (4 oz) leftover cooked chicken, diced (optional)

2–3 tablespoons chopped fresh parsley, to garnish

I have wonderful memories of my Grandma's soups, particularly this one. She would always finish it off with a good sprinkling of chopped fresh parsley – which I thought was pretty exotic at the time! This is my version, and I like to put in rice to give the soup more body. To make it extra special, use a rich stock made with a whole chicken and chop up some of the chicken to put into the soup – the secret of a good broth is the stock.

1 Put the stock into a large pan with the rice and vegetables. Season lightly with salt and pepper, cover and bring to the boil. Turn down the heat and simmer, half-covered, for 35–40 minutes.

2 Taste the soup and season again if necessary, adding a squeeze of lemon juice – this will really bring out the chicken flavour. Stir in the chicken, if using, and ladle into warm soup bowls. Sprinkle with parsley and serve scalding hot as my Grandma always did! The soup tastes even better if it's left to cool and then reheated the next day. It also freezes well.

# 11 Char-grilled Chicken and Sweetcorn Chowder

| Quick and easy |
| --- |
| Preparation time 20 minutes |
| Serves 6 |

3 small boneless, skinless chicken breasts

1 chicken stock cube, crumbled

3 whole corn cobs, stripped of their outer green husks and silky threads

2 red peppers, quartered and seeded

oil, for brushing

50 g (2 oz) butter

125 g (4½ oz) lardons (*cubetti di pancetta*)

2 onions, finely chopped

25 g (1 oz) plain flour

300 ml (½ pint) milk

400 g can black-eyed beans, drained

4 tablespoons double cream

freshly ground sea salt and freshly ground black pepper

4 tablespoons chopped fresh parsley or coriander

I love the smoky richness that char-grilling the sweetcorn and peppers brings to this soup. Sweetcorn and chicken have a real affinity and are made for each other in my variation of an American chowder. Of course you can use a can of sweetcorn for convenience but I prefer to get the barbie out – or at least the ridged griddle pan – and start those juices caramelizing. This really is a meal in a bowl.

1 Lay the chicken breasts, former skin-sides up, in a wide shallow pan and cover with cold water and the crumbled stock cube. Bring up to just under boiling point then turn the heat down to a bare simmer. Poach the chicken breasts like this for 8–10 minutes, depending on their size.

2 While the chicken is poaching, brush the corn cobs and peppers lightly with oil and barbecue them over medium coals or griddle them until the cobs are dark mahogany brown and the peppers are soft – about 10 minutes. Remove to a dish.

3 When the chicken is almost done, lift out with a slotted spoon, transfer to a plate and reserve the poaching liquid. Brush the nearly cooked chicken lightly with oil and finish on the barbecue or griddle pan.

4 Take a sharp knife and cut the kernels off the corn.

5 Melt the butter in a pan, add the lardons and cook for about 3 minutes until they are just beginning to brown. Add the onions and cook for about 5 minutes, until softened. Stir in the flour and cook for 1 minute, stirring all the while. Whisk in the reserved poaching liquid and bring to the boil, stirring until it thickens. Add the milk, black-eyed beans, corn kernels and chopped peppers, bring back to a simmer and cook for 5 minutes.

6 Roughly chop the chicken and stir into the soup, along with the cream and half the parsley or coriander. Season to taste. Heat for another 5 minutes and then serve piping hot, garnished with the remaining parsley or coriander.

# 12 Chicken and Soba Noodle Soup

| Quick and easy |
| --- |
| Preparation time 12 minutes |
| Serves 4 |

1 tablespoon sunflower oil

200 g (7 oz) shiitake mushrooms, finely sliced

2 garlic cloves, finely chopped

1 tablespoon finely chopped fresh root ginger (or grate the ginger on a Microplane grater)

1 fresh red chilli, finely sliced, seeds and all

1.2 litres (2 pints) Light Chicken Stock (see page 14)

1–2 tablespoons light soy sauce (preferably Japanese)

1–2 tablespoons runny honey

200 g (7 oz) soba noodles

6 spring onions, sliced thinly diagonally

1 tablespoon Thai fish sauce (*nam pla*)

1 lime, quartered

freshly ground sea salt

200 g (7 oz) cold cooked chicken, skinned and pulled into long shreds

2–3 tablespoons roughly chopped fresh chives or garlic chives

long chives, to garnish

During my travels around the Far East, I tasted noodle soups in countries as diverse as Singapore, Hong Kong, Indonesia and Vietnam. All had regional variants but all had one thing in common – this wonderful balance of hot, sweet, salty and sour flavours, essential in a good Asian broth. Don't be afraid to be lavish with the seasoning as these soups should have a real punchy flavour. I sometimes add roughly quartered pak choi to heat up in the broth at the end – it gives a nice crunch.

**1** Heat the sunflower oil in a large saucepan and add the mushrooms, garlic, ginger and chilli. Fry over a medium heat for 1–2 minutes, until the mushrooms start to soften.

**2** Add the stock and bring to the boil. Next add a tablespoon each of the soy sauce and honey, stir through and add the soba noodles, cooking as per the packet instructions. (Add more honey and/or soy sauce at the end if you think the soup needs it.)

**3** When the noodles are almost cooked, add the spring onions and fish sauce. Squeeze the lime quarters into the broth and then drop them into the soup.

**4** Taste and adjust the balance of hot, sweet, salt and sour. Add the chicken shreds and chopped chives or garlic chives and reheat. Ladle into warm bowls, making sure each person gets a lime quarter, and garnish with long chives.

# 13 Cream of Chicken Soup

| Informal supper |
| --- |
| Preparation time 35 minutes |
| Serves 4 |

850 ml (1½ pints) Light Chicken Stock (see page 14)

50 g (2 oz) long-grain rice

1 celery stick, thinly sliced

1 onion, chopped

a handful of parsley stalks

2 x 175–200 g (6–7 oz) ready-cooked chicken thighs, skinned, boned and diced

300 ml (½ pint) double cream

½ teaspoon chopped fresh thyme

finely grated rind of ½ small lemon

freshly ground sea salt, freshly ground black pepper and freshly grated nutmeg

2 tablespoons finely chopped fresh parsley, to garnish

I don't really know why, but in our house we always had this on high days and holidays (I suppose chicken and cream were luxury ingredients then). It's fair to say that the final result bears no resemblance to the almost caramelized taste of the popular canned versions, produced by the heat treatment of the cans. This needs a really good stock – use a cube for another dish, this needs the real deal. Buy ready-cooked chicken thighs for this, as they add a great depth of flavour to the soup.

**1** Put the stock in a large pan with the rice, celery, onion and parsley stalks. Bring to the boil, then turn down and simmer for 20 minutes or until the rice is cooked.

**2** Fish out the parsley stalks. Add the diced cooked chicken, cream, thyme and lemon rind to the stock and season to taste with salt, pepper and nutmeg. Bring to the boil and then turn down and simmer for about 8 minutes.

**3** Remove from the heat and allow to cool for 5 minutes. Then pour into a liquidizer and blitz until smooth. Reheat, taste and check the seasoning, and serve garnished with the parsley.

**NB** To get that lovely silky feel, I always pass the soup through a chinois or fine sieve, pushing it through with a ladle, which will remove all the fine fibres and leave the soup silky smooth.

# 14 Cock-a-Leekie

| |
|---|
| Informal supper |
| Preparation time 2¾ hours |
| Serves 6 |

**1.5 kg (3 lb 5 oz) oven-ready chicken (with giblets if possible)**

**450 g (1 lb) chicken wings**

**2 onions, quartered**

**900 g (2 lb) leeks, split and thoroughly washed**

**2 bay leaves**

**½ teaspoon black peppercorns**

**12 mi-cuit or no-need-to-soak prunes, stoned**

**freshly ground sea salt and freshly ground black pepper**

**a small bunch of flatleaf parsley**

This really is one of the best soups to come out of Scotland. It is a typical one-pot soup that used to be made with a boiling fowl (a tough old bird), slowly simmered with leeks from the garden to make a rich broth. Our roasting chickens are not as flavoursome as an old-fashioned boiling fowl, so I like to add some chicken wings to improve the flavour.

I don't like really soggy leeks in my soup, so I cook some with the broth and add some at the end for colour and extra texture. I really like prunes in my Cock-a-Leekie – they add richness. I tend to use soft plump mi-cuit (no-need-to-soak) prunes from Agen in France.

**1** Put the chicken, giblets, if using, and chicken wings into a large pan with the onions, half the leeks, the bay leaves, peppercorns and 2.25 litres (3½ pints) cold water. Bring to the boil, turn down the heat, and simmer very gently for 1½–2 hours.

**2** Meanwhile, cut off the green part of the remaining leeks, slice very finely and keep in a plastic bag. Slice the white parts into 1 cm (½ inch) slices and pop in a plastic bag.

**3** When the chicken is cooked, lift the whole bird out on to a tray to cool slightly. Skim any fat off the surface of the stock and then strain the stock and chicken wings through a colander into a bowl. Rinse out the pan and strain the stock back into it through a fine sieve.

**4** Add the prunes and the sliced green leek to the stock, bring back to the boil and simmer for about 10 minutes. Then add the white of leek and simmer for 15 minutes. Taste and check the seasoning and add the parsley.

**5** Carve off as much chicken as you would like in the soup (don't forget the wings) and cut or tear it into pieces, reserving the rest for another dish. Add the chicken to the soup, heat through and serve.

# 15 Hot and Sour Soup with Minced Chicken Dumplings

<table>
<tr><td>Low fat</td></tr>
<tr><td>Preparation time 25 minutes</td></tr>
<tr><td>Serves 4</td></tr>
</table>

1 large stem of lemon grass

1.2 litres (2 pints) Light Chicken Stock (see page 14)

2–3 teaspoons Thai red curry paste (depending on how hot you like it)

2 shallots, finely chopped

100 g (4 oz) shiitake mushrooms, sliced

2 teaspoons light muscovado sugar

2 teaspoons Thai fish sauce (*nam pla*)

juice of 2 limes

freshly ground sea salt and freshly ground black pepper

## FOR THE DUMPLINGS:

225 g (8 oz) boneless, skinless chicken breasts, trimmed and roughly chopped

1 cm (1/2 inch) piece of fresh root ginger, peeled and finely grated

1 shallot, roughly chopped

1 egg white

## TO SERVE:

2 spring onions, finely shredded

1 red chilli, finely sliced

a handful of fresh coriander

Ainsley Harriott demonstrated this soup at the Glasgow Foodfest – it was so simple and healthy, I was hooked. I've added chicken dumplings to make it more of a meal. These dumplings are really the filling for wontons and, if feeling really fancy, you could make wontons (see page 101) and poach them in the soup.

This makes a great lunch dish. You could try making the soup with prawns, diced or minced pork or, for an extra-low-fat version, double the vegetables.

1 To make the dumplings, place the chicken, ginger, shallots, egg white and a little salt and pepper in a food processor and process until smooth. Remove the mix from the bowl and form into 20 balls. Place the dumplings on a plate. Cover and chill.

2 For the soup, smash the lemon grass stem with a rolling pin and place in a pan, with the stock, curry paste and shallots. Bring to the boil. Add the mushrooms to the pan and leave to simmer for 8–10 minutes.

3 Stir the sugar and fish sauce into the soup and carefully add the chicken dumplings. Simmer for 3–4 minutes, until the dumplings are cooked. Squeeze in the lime juice and season to taste.

4 Ladle the soup into warmed bowls and place five dumplings in each. Scatter with the spring onions, chilli and coriander and serve.

# 16 Pressed Terrine of Potato, Chicken Livers and Parma Ham

| Smart entertaining |
| Preparation time 1 hour, plus chilling time |
| Serves 12 |

2 x 225 g (8 oz) floury potatoes, such as Golden Wonder, King Edwards or Kerr's Pinks

8 thin slices of Parma ham

175 g (6 oz) butter

2 garlic cloves, finely chopped

3 tablespoons chopped fresh flatleaf parsley

freshly ground sea salt and freshly ground black pepper

2 tablespoons sunflower oil, plus extra for oiling

750 g (1½ lb) fresh chicken livers, trimmed

25 g (1 oz) fresh Parmesan cheese, grated

300 g (10 oz) mixed baby salad leaves, dressed with a drizzle of extra virgin olive oil, to serve

This is a bit of a culinary triumph – the idea had been floating round in my head ever since I tasted a potato and *foie gras* terrine at a posh French restaurant years ago. It's now one of the dishes I'm most proud of and I think it justifies the price of this book on its own! It's the ideal dinner-party starter as it's all done in advance and will guarantee lots of 'oohs' and 'aahs'! It's a little bit tricky – the secret is in cooking the potatoes just right – they are cooked in their skins to hold them together and make slicing easier. Once made it's a cinch to serve. If you have trouble slicing it, try an electric knife.

1 You need to prepare this terrine the day before you want to serve it. First thing in the morning, boil the whole, unpeeled potatoes in salted water for 30–40 minutes, until tender when pierced with a skewer. Drain them, leave to go cold and then chill them in the fridge for quite a few hours.

2 Lightly oil a 7.5 cm (3 inch) deep, 7.5 x 25 cm (3 x 10 inch) terrine dish and then line it with some cling film, leaving a lot overhanging. Now line the dish with the slices of Parma ham, overlapping them slightly and leaving about 7.5 cm (3 inches) overhanging all the way round.

3 Peel the potatoes and cut each one into 5 mm (¼ inch) slices. Melt the butter with the garlic in a small pan and leave to cook over a gentle heat for 10 minutes. Stir in the parsley and plenty of seasoning and set aside to cool but not set.

4 Heat half the sunflower oil in a large frying pan, add half the chicken livers and fry them over a high heat, turning them every now and then, for 2–3 minutes until nicely browned but still rare and juicy in the centre. Season well with salt and pepper and set aside while you cook the rest.

5 To assemble the terrine, pour a thin layer of the garlic butter into the bottom of the dish and tilt it back and forth until it has completely covered the Parma ham-lined base. Now layer one-third of the potatoes, then half the chicken livers and sprinkle with half the Parmesan. Spoon over some more of the garlic butter and repeat these layers once more, remembering to season them as you go. Now cover the top of the terrine with the remaining one-third of the sliced potatoes and then fold over the Parma ham so the potatoes are completely covered.

**6** Fold over the cling film so the terrine is completely covered. Weight it down by placing a second terrine dish on top and filling it with heavy objects. Slide it into the fridge and leave to chill overnight.

**7** When ready to serve, fold the cling film back from the top of the terrine and invert it on to a board or serving dish. Using a very sharp knife, carve it into 12 thin slices and place them on plates. Pile the dressed salad leaves alongside, drizzle around the remaining herb oil and serve, perhaps with some crusty bread.

# 17 Stracciatella (Italian Chicken Broth)

| Smart entertaining |
| --- |
| Preparation time 20 minutes |
| Serves 6 |

**6 eggs**

**50 g (2 oz) Parmesan cheese, grated**

**a good grating of nutmeg**

**1 teaspoon finely grated lemon rind**

**freshly ground sea salt and freshly ground black pepper**

**1.5 litres (2¾ pints) Light Chicken Stock (see page 14) or canned chicken consommé**

**a squeeze of lemon juice**

The wonderful Maxine Clark, who teaches classes at Nairns Cook School, demonstrated this soup amongst other Italian regional dishes. It is so simple and, if made with a proper chicken stock, it is fantastic. A stock cube won't do here but canned chicken consommé would work. The soup originates from Rome – *stracciatella* means 'rags'. And if you get it right, you will have just that – little raggy bits of egg floating in the soup. Using a fork instead of a whisk will help create the correct texture. I must admit the only time I had this in Italy it was just a mush, so it was a bit of a revelation to taste this one!

**1** Using a fork, beat the eggs really well with the Parmesan, nutmeg and grated lemon rind. Season with salt and pepper.

**2** Bring the stock or consommé to the boil. When it has reached a good rolling boil, pour in the egg mixture, a little at a time, whisking with a fork. Once all the egg is added, turn down the heat and simmer for 5 minutes, whisking occasionally with the fork (you don't want big lumps of egg here). Season again and add a squeeze of lemon juice. You should end up with a creamy-looking cloudy soup full of little egg threads. This is a great soup to cook when you are feeling a bit the worse for wear!

# 18 Bruschetta of Chicken Livers with Chilli Jam

| Informal supper |
| --- |
| Preparation time 30 minutes |
| Serves 4 |

**4 large thick slices of *pain de campagne*, or sourdough, or a halved and split ciabatta loaf**

**1 tablespoon olive oil, plus extra for brushing**

**1 garlic clove, halved lengthways**

**450 g (1 lb) fresh chicken livers, trimmed**

**freshly ground sea salt and freshly ground black pepper**

**200 g (7 oz) rocket or watercress**

**1 small red onion, really thinly sliced**

**FOR THE CHILLI JAM:**

**400 g can chopped Italian plum tomatoes**

**1–2 bird's eye chillies, halved, seeded and finely sliced**

**3 garlic cloves, finely chopped**

**1 tablespoon balsamic vinegar**

**350 g (12 oz) sugar**

This is exactly the sort of thing I like to have for an indulgent summer lunch. I say indulgent because chicken livers taste so good it does feel like a treat – and a cheap one at that! To make the best bruschetta, good firm bread is a must – *pain de campagne*, sourdough, a home-made crusty loaf or even ciabatta. Soft, pappy bread will never work. When grilling bruschetta it's important to brush the bread with olive oil to stop it sticking to the griddle. The chilli jam is a cinch to make, goes with almost anything and keeps for ages.

**1** First make the chilli jam. Put all the ingredients into a pan, stir to help the sugar dissolve and then bring slowly to the boil. Turn down the heat and simmer gently for about 20 minutes or until reduced and slightly thickened (it will thicken even more when cold). Store in a sterilized jar (to sterilize, submerge the jar in boiling water for 5 minutes) in the fridge for up to four weeks. Remember to keep refrigerated once opened.

**2** Heat a griddle pan to medium heat. Brush the bread slices with olive oil and place on the griddle for 1–2 minutes each side until nice and crisp. A word of warning: keep an eye on the temperature – if it's too hot you'll end up with scorched bread before it has a chance to crisp up. If you don't have a griddle pan, don't worry; simply bake the slices in a moderate oven for 3–4 minutes. When they're ready, rub a cut clove of garlic over the surface of each slice.

**3** Heat a large frying pan until very hot and add the olive oil. Season the chicken livers well with salt and pepper. Add them to the pan (don't crowd the pan – cook the livers in batches if your frying pan is not very large) and cook for just 1 minute on each side – you want the outsides to become lightly browned but the insides to remain pink and juicy.

**4** Place each bruschetta on a serving plate and divide the rocket or watercress between them. Sprinkle over some red onion slices and top with the chicken livers. Spoon some chilli jam over the livers and serve immediately.

# 19 Chicken Liver Pâté

| Prepare in advance |
| --- |
| Preparation time 30 minutes |
| Serves 6 |

300 g (10 oz) butter, at room temperature

1 onion, finely chopped

1 carrot, finely chopped

1 celery stick, finely chopped

1 large garlic clove, finely chopped

450 g (1 lb) chicken livers

1 tablespoon chopped fresh lemon thyme, plus sprigs to garnish

a splash of tawny port, Madeira, sherry or dry vermouth

freshly ground sea salt and freshly ground black pepper

Clarified Butter (see page 18)

I have fond memories of chicken liver pâté from the days when I was starting to cook – it was a staple. I made it again recently and wondered why it had ever gone out of fashion because it really is fantastic and very easy to make. It's perfect served with some pickled gherkins or capers as a snack or first course – eat the pâté on hot toast so that it melts a bit. Frozen livers will do for this.

**1** Melt 25 g (1 oz) of the butter in a large frying pan and cook the onion, carrot, celery and garlic over a low heat until meltingly soft (about 20 minutes). When they are soft, use a slotted spoon to place them in the bowl of your food processor.

**2** While they are cooking, trim the chicken livers of any gristle and cut off any discoloured bits. Pat dry on kitchen paper.

**3** Heat the pan again, add the livers and 15 g (½ oz) of the butter and fry over a high heat, turning them as they brown, for about 3 minutes until they are nicely browned and crisp on the outside but still pink and juicy in the middle. Add the lemon thyme and a splash of your chosen tipple, let it all bubble for a minute and then tip the livers into the food processor with the vegetables and season with salt and pepper.

**4** Chuck in the remaining butter and blitz in pulses until fairly smooth – I like a bit of texture, this is not a smooth parfait!

**5** Scrape the pâté out into a large earthenware bowl or spoon it into individual bowls, smooth the top, scatter with the sprigs of thyme and pour over a thin layer of clarified butter. It keeps for ages in the fridge once it's covered with the clarified butter. I like to serve it with toasted fingers of ciabatta, but remember to bring it to room temperature before serving – fridge-cold pâté will not do!

# 20 Italian Chicken and Roast Pepper Salad

| Prepare in advance |
| --- |
| Preparation time 1 hour 10 minutes, plus marinating time |
| Serves 4 |

1.8 kg (4 lb) chicken with giblets (free-range if possible)

1 carrot

1 onion, halved

1 celery stick

2 bay leaves

1 bouquet garni

8 black peppercorns

1 large yellow pepper

1 large red pepper

200 ml (7 fl oz) good olive oil, plus 1 tablespoon for brushing the peppers

1 garlic clove, finely diced

1 small whole bird's eye chilli

100 g (4 oz) fresh flatleaf parsley leaves, picked off the stalks

freshly ground sea salt and freshly ground black pepper

This is one of those great make-ahead dishes where the flavours improve with keeping. It's based on a medieval Italian recipe for cooking a capon to make it tender and juicy. After poaching the chicken you have a wonderful stock to freeze for making soup later. The combination of perfectly poached chicken, caramelized, silky-smooth roast peppers and olive oil is very seductive. Perfect picnic food!

**1** Place the chicken in a large pan and add all the giblets except the liver, which you can reserve and freeze. Add the carrot, onion, celery, bay leaves, bouquet garni and peppercorns. Cover with cold water and slowly bring to the boil. Turn the heat down and simmer gently for about 1 hour or until tender.

**2** Meanwhile, preheat the oven to 190°C/375°/Gas Mark 5. Halve the peppers lengthways and arrange them, cut-sides down, in a roasting pan. Brush all over with 1 tablespoon olive oil. Roast for about 30 minutes, until the peppers start to collapse and blacken around the edges. Remove the peppers, place in a bowl, cover tightly with cling film and leave for 15 minutes. Then remove the skins, which should slip off quite easily. Set aside.

**3** Drain and reserve the stock, and freeze to use later. Cool the chicken completely then remove the flesh in large pieces, discarding skin and bones. (You can use the skin and bones to enrich the stock and simmer for another hour if you have the time.) Tear the chicken into shreds or strips and place in a large bowl.

**4** Heat the oil in a small pan and add the garlic and chilli. Cook gently until the garlic begins to release its pungent smell (but doesn't brown) and then pour over the chicken. Mix well, cover and place in the refrigerator to marinate for several hours or overnight.

**5** The next day, stir in the peppers and parsley, season with salt and pepper and serve at room temperature.

# 21 Warm Salad of Crispy Chicken Thighs

| |
|---|
| Informal supper |
| Preparation time 50 minutes |
| Serves 4 |

75 g (3 oz) mooli or daikon

1 small carrot

4 spring onions

freshly ground sea salt and freshly ground black pepper

4 boneless chicken thighs, each weighing about 100 g (4 oz), with skin left on

1 tablespoon lemon juice

1 small, ripe mango

50 g (2 oz) mangetout, shredded

50 g (2 oz) fresh beansprouts

a handful of fresh coriander leaves, washed

200 g bag of mixed small salad leaves, e.g. mizuna, watercress, lamb's lettuce, etc., washed

50 g (2 oz) cashew nuts, crushed

1 red chilli, halved, seeded and finely shredded

**FOR THE SWEET CHILLI VINAIGRETTE:**

3 tablespoons sunflower oil

4 tablespoons rice wine vinegar or white wine vinegar

2 tablespoons sweet chilli sauce

1 tablespoon *furikake* (Japanese seasoning, optional)

1 tablespoon light sesame oil

This is my all-time favourite salad – everything works perfectly together and the method of cooking the chicken thighs is simply the best ever. Chicken legs and thighs are not only cheaper than breasts but are much tastier as well. The secret is in the long, slow cooking, which would leave a breast fillet dry and tasteless but, using thighs, you end up with unbelievably crispy skin – a bit like crackling – and succulent, well-flavoured flesh.

**1** Fill a bowl with water and add a load of ice cubes. Shave long, thin strips off the mooli and carrot with a potato peeler and put them into the water. Cut the spring onions into long shreds and add them to the water. Leave to firm up and curl in the fridge for 20 minutes, then drain well and pat dry.

**2** Meanwhile, heat a medium-sized non-stick frying pan over a medium to low heat. Season the thighs well, then place them in the pan, skin-sides down (they should fit the pan snugly). Now cook the thighs without moving or turning them until the skin is nice and crispy. This will take about 30 minutes – so keep an eye on the pan and turn the heat down if the thighs are sizzling too much. They should sizzle slowly. Turn over the thighs, which will be well browned by now, and continue to cook for another 2–3 minutes. Add the lemon juice and shake the pan to make sure it is evenly distributed. Cook for another 3 minutes, then remove to a warm place to rest for 5 minutes.

**3** Halve the mango past each side of the stone and peel using a potato peeler. Slice each half into long, thin slices. Put the drained vegetables into a bowl with the mango. Add the mangetout, beansprouts, coriander, salad leaves, cashew nuts and chilli and lightly toss together with your hands. Lastly, whisk the vinaigrette ingredients together and assemble the salad.

**4** Place a generous handful of the oriental salad in the centre of each plate and divide the chicken thighs between them. Drizzle over some dressing and serve.

# 22 Chicken Salad with Feta Cheese, Rosemary and Lemon

| Informal supper |
| --- |
| Preparation time 1 hour 20 minutes |
| Serves 4 |

1.5 kg (3 lb 5 oz) free-range chicken

50 g (2 oz) butter

1 lemon, cut into wedges

4–5 garlic cloves, lightly crushed

freshly ground sea salt and freshly ground black pepper

175 g (6 oz) feta cheese, crumbled into small pieces

200 g (7 oz) cherry tomatoes, halved

leaves from a sprig of fresh rosemary, very finely chopped

50 ml (2 fl oz) olive oil, plus extra to serve

finely grated rind of 1 lemon

3 tablespoons lemon juice

dressed salad leaves and olive oil, or slices of grilled bread or toast, to serve

This recipe is ideal for using up cold roast chicken. So good is it that I often find myself roasting a chicken specifically for this salad, which is perfect for a picnic or an alfresco summer lunch, or as a winter starter to remind you of summer. It relies on good ingredients to make a simple dish great. Try to get a free-range or organic chicken to roast and buy the best feta you can find. This is definitely an excuse to use your top-of-the-range olive oil – and is another dish you can make a day in advance as the flavours only improve.

1 Try to roast the chicken a day ahead. Preheat the oven to 200°C/400°F/Gas Mark 6. Untruss the chicken and slash through the skin joining the legs to the breasts. Let them flop open to ensure even cooking. Allow the chicken to come to cool room temperature. Push your fingers between the chicken breasts and the skin to make two pockets. Stuff 15 g (½ oz) of the butter into each one and rub the remaining butter all over the outside of the skin. Stuff the cavity with the lemon wedges and garlic. Season very well and put the bird on a wire rack over a roasting tin. Splash 3 tablespoons water into the tin and bang the chicken in the oven to roast until well browned, about 1 hour, basting occasionally.

2 Depending on your oven, you might need to cover the chicken loosely with a sheet of foil after about 40 minutes to stop it overbrowning. Test with a skewer in the thickest part of the thigh: the juices should run clear.

3 Leave until cold, then pull off the legs and use a knife to cut off the breasts. Track down the two 'oysters' on the underside of the bird (these are little secret crackers of flesh). Using your fingers, flake the flesh off the breasts, thighs and drumsticks. Try to get nice long strands and don't forget the skin.

4 Pile all the flaked chicken (and 'oysters', if you haven't eaten them already) into a large mixing bowl and add the crumbled feta and cherry tomatoes. Whisk together the rosemary, olive oil, lemon rind and juice and some seasoning and add this to the bowl. Toss well, check the seasoning and keep cold until needed.

5 Serve with a few dressed salad leaves and a drizzle of olive oil, or pile on to slices of grilled bread or toast.

# 23 Smoked Chicken Caesar Salad

| Prepare in advance |
| --- |
| Preparation time 45 minutes |
| Serves 4 |

**FOR THE CROÛTONS:**

3 tablespoons olive oil

1 garlic clove, crushed

2 slices of bread, 5 mm (¼ inch) thick, crusts removed, crumb cubed

freshly ground sea salt and freshly ground black pepper

**FOR THE CAESAR DRESSING:**

1 small can anchovies in oil, drained and finely chopped

2 garlic cloves, crushed

juice of 1 lemon

2 tablespoons mayonnaise

75 ml (2½ fl oz) olive oil

**FOR THE SALAD:**

2 romaine or cos lettuces

8 cherry tomatoes, halved

1 smoked chicken or 2 smoked chicken breasts

2 ripe avocados

100 g (4 oz) Parmesan cheese shavings

I got the idea for this from the highly talented Keith and Nicola Braidwood, who own and run the wonderful Braidwood's restaurant in Dalry, North Ayrshire (well worth a visit). This dish really relies on sourcing well-smoked, still succulent chicken. Avoid the ones that look as if they have been painted with dark brown varnish – some are actually painted with a smoke flavouring! Good lettuce is essential and I use romaine hearts or cos lettuce – you have to get the ratio of stem to green just right for the best crunch.

**1** First make the croûtons. Warm a frying pan through (but not too hot). Add the olive oil and garlic. Allow to infuse on a very low heat for about 5 minutes. Drop the cubes of bread into the pan and fry gently, stirring from time to time with a wooden spoon. After 10–15 minutes, the croûtons should be golden brown. Season with salt and pepper, then remove the croûtons from the pan and allow to drain on kitchen paper. Discard the garlic.

**2** To make the dressing, place the chopped anchovies, garlic, lemon juice and mayonnaise in a small bowl. Slowly whisk in the olive oil and then 3 tablespoons cold water.

**3** Remove any damaged leaves from the lettuces. Separate the leaves and wash well. Drain and pat dry. Roughly chop the leaves and toss with the croûtons and halved tomatoes.

**4** Slice the smoked chicken. Halve the avocados, then remove the stones. Peel and slice evenly, then add to the salad with the dressing. Season and toss gently.

**5** To serve, divide the salad between four plates, scatter with the Parmesan shavings and serve.

# 24 Warm Salad of Lemon Chicken

| |
|---|
| Smart entertaining |
| Preparation 20 minutes, plus marinating time |
| Serves 4 as a starter |

**2 boneless, skinless chicken breasts**

**finely grated rind of 1 unwaxed lemon**

**2 tablespoons Chilli Oil (see below)**

**1 garllc clove, crushed**

**freshly ground sea salt and freshly ground black pepper**

**2 tablespoons sunflower oil**

**juice of ½ lemon**

**TO SERVE:**

**200 g (7 oz) dressed salad leaves, chilled**

**Parmesan cheese shavings**

The secret of this recipe is to cut the chicken into thin escalopes, which allows the marinade to penetrate the flesh fully. This means it's extremely important to cook the escalopes just right. Use a searingly hot pan, not too crowded, and cook them on one side for just a minute, or the chicken will stew, cook for too long and dry out.

This recipe cries out for my favourite kitchen gadget, a fine Microplane grater, which has transformed a chore – grating lemon rind – into a pleasure! When cooked, the lemon zest almost caramelizes. The lemons must be unwaxed and, for variation, try using orange or lime instead.

**1** You can marinate the chicken for 1–6 hours before cooking. Remove any sinew from each breast and pull off the long breast fillet. Using a sharp knife cut thin – 3 mm (⅛ inch) – slices of chicken across the grain. Cut each fillet into three pieces and you should have 25–30 escalopes. Place them in a small bowl and grate the lemon rind directly on to the chicken. Add the chilli oil and garlic and season with pepper. Cover with cling film and refrigerate until you are ready to cook.

**2** Heat a large frying pan until it is very hot indeed. Add the sunflower oil and throw in as many chicken escalopes as will comfortably fit the base of the pan. Cook really quickly over a high heat so that the escalopes become crisp along the edges. Tip out on to a plate and season before reheating the pan and cooking the rest. Put the cooked chicken back in the pan and squeeze over the lemon juice. Shake the pan to coat the chicken pieces evenly.

**3** Place the chilled salad leaves in four bowls. Divide the chicken escalopes between the bowls and scatter over a few Parmesan shavings.

## Chilli Oil

This oil is hot, so don't fry anything with it! Slice 225 g (8 oz) fresh chillies in half, lengthways, and place in a pan. Pour on 1 litre (1¾ pints) sunflower oil and bring to the boil. Simmer gently for 5 minutes, remove from the heat and allow to cool (this takes approximately 2 hours). Once cooled, transfer the chillies and oil to a plastic tub and store in a cool place for 2–3 weeks. Pour the oil through a sieve to remove the chillies before using it (or your oil will be too hot). I usually keep the chilli oil in an old olive oil bottle, but remember to label it well. A skull and crossbones will suffice.

# 25 Bang Bang Chicken

| Quick and easy |
| --- |
| Preparation time 30 minutes, plus cooling time |
| Serves 4 |

450 g (1 lb) boneless, skinless chicken breasts

chicken stock or cold water

seasonings, to taste
(see method)

**FOR THE PEANUT DRESSING:**

3–4 tablespoons smooth peanut butter (or tahini)

2 tablespoons light soy sauce (preferably Japanese)

2 teaspoons Worcestershire sauce (this adds a nice kick!)

1 tablespoon sake or dry sherry

1 teaspoon sesame oil

1 teaspoon sugar

1 teaspoon ground roasted Sichuan peppercorns

a good pinch of cayenne pepper or chilli powder

a small knob of fresh root ginger, peeled and finely grated

**TO SERVE:**

1 large cucumber

½ bunch of spring onions, thinly shredded diagonally

I've seen many travesties of this famous Sichuan dish, including one using mayonnaise and tomato ketchup. It takes its name from the wooden 'pang' or stick used to beat the cooked chicken to loosen the fibres. Beating the cooked chicken allows the fibres to separate more easily and be torn into the long strips characteristic of the dish. Traditionally, sesame-seed paste (tahini) is used but I prefer smooth peanut butter for ease. Of course you can use cooked chicken breasts for speed. This can be made the day before – as the chicken absorbs the flavours from the peanut dressing the flavour improves – and makes a great filling for a wrap. You can also serve it with glass noodles.

**1** Lay the chicken breasts, former skin-sides up, in a shallow wide pan and cover with stock or cold water (at this stage you can add all sorts of seasonings if you want – peppercorns, bay leaves, herbs, wine). Bring up to just under boiling point and then turn the heat down to a bare simmer. Poach the chicken breasts for 10–12 minutes depending on size. Lift them out with a slotted spoon and transfer to a plate to cool completely.

**2** Now make the dressing. Whisk all the ingredients together and set aside.

**3** Scrub the cucumber under hot water to remove any waxy deposits. Chop off the ends, cut in half and scrape out all the seeds. Slice as thinly as you can or cut into long shreds, cover and set aside.

**4** Lay the chicken breasts on a chopping board, cover with cling film, and give them a light bash all over with a rolling pin to loosen the fibres. Pull and tear the chicken into long strips. Dump this into the dressing and toss well to coat.

**5** Arrange the chicken with the cucumber on a big plate and scatter over the spring onions.

# 26 Char-grilled Chicken with Roast Vegetable Couscous

| |
|---|
| Smart entertaining |
| Preparation time 30 minutes |
| Serves 4 |

1 aubergine, sliced lengthways, salted and allowed to drain

2 courgettes, each cut lengthways into 4 slices

1 red pepper, halved, seeded and cut into 4 strips

3 tablespoons olive oil, plus extra for coating

freshly ground sea salt and freshly ground black pepper

4 boneless, skinless chicken breasts

250 g (9 oz) couscous

2 tablespoons chopped fresh coriander

juice of 1 lemon

I love this dish. It's cheap and easy enough for a lunchtime treat, yet can easily transform into a dinner-party winner. Couscous can be boring and bland but here it's bursting with the flavours of the Mediterranean – sweet char-grilled vegetables, lemon and lots of fresh herbs. I always add plenty of olive oil to the couscous, to make sure it's nice and moist, and drizzle some around the finished dish to serve.

Most of the work for this dish can be done in advance, including the couscous, which can be reheated in the oven, or even better – the microwave. For a dinner party, a little Sauce Vierge (see page 20) would really make it special.

1 Heat a ribbed griddle pan until hot. Coat all the vegetables in olive oil and add them to the pan in batches. Char-grill for about 5 minutes on each side until each strip has griddle marks on it and is nice and tender. Remove from the pan, season with salt and pepper and set aside while you cook the chicken.

2 Brush the chicken breasts with olive oil and ensure the griddle pan is hot. Place the chicken breasts on it and cook them for 2 minutes without touching them. Rotate the breasts through 90 degrees and cook for another 2 minutes. This will give a great criss-cross pattern on the flesh. Turn the breasts over and cook for a further 4 minutes or until cooked through, turning after 2 minutes to get the same criss-cross pattern on this side. Leave on a warm plate to rest.

3 To make the couscous, pour the boiling water over the grains and cover with cling film. After 5 minutes, remove the cling film and, using a fork, fluff up the grains so that they separate. Now dice the char-grilled vegetables and stir through the couscous, with the coriander, 3 tablespoons of olive oil, lemon juice and some seasoning.

4 Carve the rested breasts into four slices each. Divide the couscous between four plates and top with the carved char-grilled breasts.

# 27 Coronation Chicken

| Quick and easy |
|---|
| Preparation time 25 minutes |
| Serves 4 |

1 medium (1.3 kg/3 lb) poached chicken (see page 14), its flesh stripped into bite-sized pieces

**FOR THE SAUCE:**

1 small onion, chopped

2 teaspoons vegetable oil

2 teaspoons curry paste

1/2 teaspoon tomato purée

1 small bay leaf

75 ml (2 1/2 fl oz) red wine

2 teaspoons apricot jam

1 slice of lemon

1 teaspoon lemon juice

freshly ground sea salt and freshly ground black pepper

300 ml (1/2 pint) mayonnaise

2 tablespoons double cream

Everybody loves coronation chicken if it is made well, but it has become a bit of a low-rent classic, alongside prawn cocktail! Sadly, there are numerous bad versions of the dish – pale shadows of the real thing invented 50 years ago by Constance Spry and Rosemary Hume of the Cordon Bleu School in London to mark the coronation celebrations of 1953. I'm giving the sauce recipe based on its classic form – nobody does it better, as they say! The sauce is used to coat the shredded flesh of a medium-sized cold poached chicken.

**1** To make the sauce, cook the onion gently for 4 minutes in the oil until softened. Add the curry paste and fry gently for 1 minute. Add the tomato purée and 3 tablespoons water, then the bay leaf, red wine, jam, lemon slice and juice, and salt and pepper, and simmer for 8 minutes.

**2** Strain the mixture, pushing as much as possible through a sieve. Use this sauce to flavour the mayonnaise to the desired strength. Half-whip the cream and stir it into the sauce.

**3** Dress the chicken pieces with the sauce and serve with salads of your choice – 50 years ago it would have been rice salad.

# 28 Warm Chicken Liver Salad with Potatoes and Lardons

| |
|---|
| Informal supper |
| Preparation time 40 minutes |
| Serves 4 |

350 g (12 oz) fresh chicken livers

2 tablespoons olive oil

2 tablespoons chopped fresh thyme

freshly ground sea salt and freshly ground black pepper

350 g (12 oz) Pink Fir Apple or Anya potatoes (or any long salad potato)

2 x 130 g packets of lardons (*cubetti di pancetta*)

3 tablespoons balsamic vinegar or sherry vinegar

3 tablespoons chopped fresh parsley, plus extra to garnish

200 g (7 oz) mixed salad leaves, to serve

I love hot, squidgy-in-the-middle livers. Firm, pink and juicy, they are quick to prepare and cook and very filling. But they have to be fresh if cooked this way, not frozen. They should be dark, firm and glossy – not watery and crumbly. To me they are a luxury item, but so cheap! It's important to get the pan searing hot, and don't overload it or the livers will stew. It's better to cook them in batches and get them nice and crisp on the outside yet pink in the middle. Just don't overcook them! Press one with your finger, it should just give – if bouncy, then it's overcooked.

**1** Trim the chicken livers of any gristle and cut off any discoloured bits. Pat dry on kitchen paper. Put into a small bowl with the olive oil, half the chopped thyme and plenty of seasoning. Leave to marinate for 15 minutes.

**2** Meanwhile, boil the potatoes in salted water for 12–15 minutes until tender. Drain and slice thickly. Return to the hot pan, cover and keep warm.

**3** Heat a non-stick frying pan and fry the lardons until golden and crisp. Tip out of the pan on to a plate and keep warm. Reheat the pan until almost smoking and then add the marinated chicken livers and fry over a high heat, turning them as they brown, for about 3 minutes until they are nicely browned and crisp on the outside but still pink and juicy in the middle. Remove the chicken livers to a plate and keep warm.

**4** Add the vinegar, parsley, remaining thyme, and salt and pepper to the frying pan and bring to the boil, scraping any brown bits from the bottom of the pan. Boil until reduced by half. Return the pancetta, chicken livers and sliced potatoes and toss well. Divide the salad leaves between four warmed plates, pile the chicken liver mixture on top, sprinkle with extra chopped parsley and eat straight away.

# 29 Chicken with Penne, Pesto and Rocket

| |
|---|
| Quick and easy |
| Preparation time 20 minutes |
| Serves 4 |

**400 g (14 oz) dried penne**

**450 g (1 lb) leftover cooked chicken**

**6 tablespoons My Home-made Pesto (see below) or really good bought stuff**

**200 g (7 oz) fresh rocket leaves**

**freshly ground sea salt and freshly ground black pepper**

**75 g (3 oz) Parmesan cheese, grated, and fresh basil leaves, to serve**

I find myself using chicken, penne and pesto together a lot, as they have a natural affinity with each other, and a dish like this one is so quick and easy to make. I love the way the pesto is sucked into the penne. My pesto has to have a bit of a crunch, so I only process it for a short time. During summer, I like to make large batches of it to freeze in ice-cube trays, turning the cubes out into a plastic box or bag. They keep for up to a year in the freezer. The best bit of this recipe is throwing the rocket in at the end to wilt into the pasta – great texture!

**1** Boil the pasta according to the manufacturer's instructions in plenty of boiling, salted water.

**2** While the pasta is boiling, shred the chicken into bite-sized pieces.

**3** When the pasta is just cooked, or really al dente, drain through a colander but keep back about 4 tablespoons of the cooking water and return the pasta to the pan with the reserved water. Stir in the chicken, cover and set over a very gentle heat for 1–2 minutes to steam and reheat the chicken properly (this is why you cook the pasta very al dente, as it will continue to cook while the chicken is reheating).

**4** Uncover, stir in the pesto so that it coats everything, then fling in the rocket, stir and let it wilt for a minute. Season with salt and pepper. Pile into warmed serving bowls, drench with grated Parmesan and add the basil leaves. Eat immediately!

**My Home-made Pesto**
Put 3 roughly chopped garlic cloves and 175 ml (6 fl oz) extra virgin olive oil in a food processor and whizz until you've got a garlicky oil. Scrape down the sides with a spatula, then add 75 g (3 oz) fresh basil, flatleaf parsley and rocket leaves and whizz until smooth. Add 50 g (2 oz) pine nuts and whizz for a few seconds until they start breaking down but the mixture is still crunchy. Lastly, grate 50 g (2 oz) Parmesan cheese and add to the mixture. Season, then process for a couple of seconds until mixed in. Don't overwork – pesto should be quite crunchy, not smooth. Scrape out into a clean jam jar, cover with a film of olive oil and keep in the fridge for up to 2 weeks, or freeze. Each time you use some of the pesto, flatten down its surface with a spoon and splash in some more oil before returning it to the fridge. This keeps the pesto sealed and stops it darkening and losing its freshness.

# 30 Fettuccine with Chicken, Mushrooms, Garlic and Cream

| |
|---|
| Informal supper |
| Preparation time 25 minutes |
| Serves 4 |

2 tablespoons olive oil

130 g packet of lardons (*cubetti di pancetta*)

1 onion, thinly sliced

1 large garlic clove, crushed

225 g (8 oz) chestnut mushrooms, sliced

a good splash of dry white wine (about 75 ml/2½ fl oz)

75 ml (2½ fl oz) Light Chicken Stock (see page 14 or you could use ½ chicken stock cube, dissolved in 75 ml/2½ fl oz boiling water)

150 ml (¼ pint) double cream

1 tablespoon finely chopped fresh tarragon

freshly ground sea salt and freshly ground black pepper

400 g (14 oz) dried fettuccine

450 g (1 lb) leftover cooked chicken, diced

Classic flavours for chicken in a gentle dish that is great comfort food. Chicken with mushrooms, garlic and cream is featured in countless dishes, quite simply because all these ingredients work so well together. This is one of my favourite recipes and, for a little extra depth, I like to add some fresh tarragon just before serving.

**1** Heat the oil in a frying pan, add the lardons and fry until they begin to crisp up around the edges. Add the onion and garlic, and cook for 2–3 minutes until the onion begins to soften. Now add the mushrooms, and cook over a medium heat for 3–4 minutes, stirring to prevent sticking.

**2** Splash in the wine and boil fast to evaporate it, then stir in the stock. Bring to the boil, pour in the cream and bring to the boil once more. Turn down the heat and simmer until the sauce reduces and thickens. Stir in the tarragon, season with salt and pepper and set aside.

**3** Cook the fettuccine according to the manufacturer's instructions and drain, keeping back 2–3 tablespoons of the cooking water. Return the pasta to the pan with the reserved water and add the chicken. Cover and cook over a gentle heat for 2–3 minutes to allow the chicken to heat through. Uncover and stir in the sauce. Serve immediately.

# 31 Pasta with Char-grilled Chicken, Courgettes and Parmesan Cream

| |
|---|
| Smart entertaining |
| Preparation time 45 minutes |
| Serves 4 |

**450 g (1 lb) boneless, skinless chicken breasts**

**1–2 tablespoons olive oil**

**freshly ground sea salt and freshly ground black pepper**

**225 g (8 oz) courgettes, thickly sliced diagonally**

**175 ml (6 fl oz) dry white wine**

**300 ml ($\frac{1}{2}$ pint) double cream**

**juice and finely grated rind of 1 lemon**

**50 g (2 oz) Parmesan cheese, grated, plus extra to serve**

**2 tablespoons each chopped fresh flatleaf parsley and basil**

**400 g (14 oz) dried tagliatelle or other thin ribbon noodles**

A heavenly recipe but not one for the calorie-counter! Made with only a few choice ingredients – chicken, courgettes, Parmesan and cream – this can be made quickly and tastes even better if all the char-grilling is done on the barbecue. Char-grilling courgettes changes their flavour completely – they become sweet and smoky, a perfect foil for the chicken and lemony Parmesan cream. Sometimes I crumble crisply grilled pancetta rashers over the top of each serving.

**1** Using a cast-iron griddle pan is the easiest way to char-grill without a barbecue. Brush the chicken breasts with some of the olive oil and season. To form the characteristic barbecued 'stripes', cook the breasts for 3–4 minutes on one side, without moving them, then rotate them through 90 degrees and cook for a further 3 minutes before repeating on the other side. The important thing is not to fiddle – once you lay the breasts on the griddle don't touch them until it's time to flip them over. Once cooked, transfer to a warm plate to rest for 5 minutes.

**2** Now brush the courgette slices with olive oil and griddle them for 2 minutes on each side; then transfer to a plate.

**3** Deglaze the griddle pan with the wine and then pour into a small pan. Add the cream and lemon rind and bring to the boil, stirring until nicely thickened. Season with salt and pepper and then stir in the Parmesan, lemon juice to taste, and the parsley and basil.

**4** Cook the pasta according the manufacturer's instructions until al dente. Drain, keeping back 2–3 tablespoons of the cooking water, then toss with the Parmesan sauce and reserved water.

**5** To serve, either carve the chicken into thick slices and stir everything into the pasta, or spoon a pile of pasta on to each plate and top with the griddled courgettes and the sliced chicken. Serve immediately, with extra Parmesan sprinkled on top.

# 32 Strozzapreti with Chicken and Roasted Tomato Sauce

| Informal supper |
| --- |
| Preparation time 45 minutes |
| Serves 4 |

**4 boneless, skinless chicken breasts**

**400 g (14 oz) strozzapreti or other twisted pasta shapes**

**olive oil, for frying**

**freshly ground sea salt and freshly ground black pepper**

**fresh basil leaves, to garnish**

**FOR THE ROASTED TOMATO SAUCE:**

**3 tablespoons olive oil**

**600 g (1 lb 5 oz) really ripe, red plum tomatoes**

**2 large garlic cloves, sliced**

**1–2 tablespoons balsamic vinegar**

**a large pinch of sugar**

**6–8 fresh large basil leaves**

Roasting tomatoes with garlic and balsamic vinegar really intensifies their flavour. I like to use plum tomatoes, as they are very fleshy, contain less water than normal tomatoes and roast really well. I always make double the quantity of sauce and freeze half for later – especially when tomatoes are in season. While the sauce is roasting, you can prepare and flash-fry the chicken, ready to pile it on to the pasta at the last moment. The short and twisted shape of strozzapreti (Italian for 'priest stranglers'!) helps the chunky sauce to cling to them.

**1** Make the sauce first. Preheat the oven to 200°C/400°F/Gas Mark 6. Pour the olive oil into a large roasting tin. Cut each tomato in half and arrange the halves, cut-sides up, in the roasting tin, scattering the garlic slices over. Sprinkle with the balsamic vinegar and season with salt and pepper. Roast for 30 minutes or until the edges of the tomatoes are slightly blackened and the tomatoes are a bit shrivelled.

**2** Remove from the oven. For a smooth sauce, scrape the whole lot into a food processor, add the sugar and basil, blitz until smooth, then pass through a sieve into a clean pan. For a chunky sauce, mash the tomatoes and garlic with the sugar and basil in the roasting tin with a potato masher. Adjust the seasoning and keep warm.

**3** Remove any sinew from each chicken breast and pull off the long breast fillet. Using a sharp knife cut thin 3 mm (⅛ inch) slices of chicken across the grain. Cut each long fillet into three pieces and you should have 25–30 escalopes. Cover and chill until ready to cook.

**4** Cook the pasta until it's al dente; then drain, keeping 2 tablespoons of the cooking water in the pan. Return the pasta to the pan with the reserved cooking water and stir in the sauce. Cover and keep warm.

**5** Heat a large frying pan until it is very hot indeed. Add 1 tablespoon olive oil and throw in as many chicken escalopes as will comfortably fit the base of the pan. Cook really quickly over a high heat so that the escalopes become crisp along their edges. Tip out on to a plate and season before cooking the rest, adding more oil and letting the pan come up to temperature as necessary.

**6** Pile the pasta into four bowls, top with the chicken, garnish with basil and serve.

# 33 Chicken Lasagne

| |
|---|
| Informal supper |
| Preparation time 50 minutes |
| Serves 4–6 |

**600 ml (1 pint) White Sauce (see page 16)**

**125 g (4½ oz) Parmesan cheese, grated**

**1 quantity Quick Tomato Sauce (see page 13)**

**olive oil, for brushing**

**450 g (1 lb) cooked chicken, shredded**

**450 g (1 lb) fresh lasagne sheets**

**green salad, to serve**

This is the ideal dish for plonking on the table and getting everyone to tuck in. It doesn't take long to prepare as there's no long, slow-cooked meat sauce. All you have to do is make a white sauce and a quick tomato sauce, ensure you have sheets of fresh lasagne, and some cooked chicken and Parmesan, and you're off! The beauty of using fresh lasagne sheets is that they don't need any pre-cooking. The whole thing can be layered up the night before and cooked the next day, and it's even better reheated the following day. A tip – keep the layers of sauces very thin or you will run out of sauce before you have finished layering the dish!

**1** Preheat the oven to 190°C/375°F/Gas Mark 5. Gently warm the white sauce and stir in half the Parmesan.

**2** Brush a 20 x 28 cm (8 x 11 inch) lasagne dish with olive oil and cover the base with shredded chicken. Spoon a little tomato sauce on top of this and then cover with lasagne. Spoon a layer of white sauce over the lasagne, then sprinkle with Parmesan cheese. Scatter with another layer of chicken and repeat these layers, ending up with a layer of pasta topped with white sauce and Parmesan.

**3** Bake for 30 minutes until brown and bubbling, then remove from the oven and allow to stand for 5 minutes before serving. Take the lasagne to the table as it is and follow with a mound of crisp green salad.

# 34 Chicken Bolognese

| Prepare in advance |
| --- |
| Preparation time 1 hour 20 minutes |
| Serves 4–6 |

2 tablespoons olive oil

1 onion, finely chopped

1 carrot, finely chopped

1 celery stick, finely chopped

2 garlic cloves, finely chopped

450 g (1 lb) minced chicken (preferably thigh meat)

1/2 teaspoon dried basil

1/2 teaspoon dried thyme

1/2 teaspoon dried marjoram

freshly ground sea salt and freshly ground black pepper

150 ml (1/4 pint) white wine

200 g can chopped tomatoes

1 teaspoon sugar

1 chicken stock cube, dissolved in 300 ml (1/2 pint) hot water

450 g (1 lb) dried spaghetti

grated Parmesan cheese, to serve

fresh basil leaves, to garnish

Minced chicken is low in fat, so make this as a healthier alternative to the usual meat-based Bolognese sauce. Mincing your own chicken from chicken thigh meat is preferable to buying ready-minced chicken, as who knows what is in there! Also, the thighs have so much flavour in them they are ideal for this robust sauce. I make the sauce lighter by adding white wine instead of red, reducing the amount of tomato and including a decent amount of vegetables. This is about the only time I advise using dried herbs – their flavour seems to burst through during the long cooking. The sauce is another good recipe to make in bulk and freeze.

1 Heat the olive oil in a medium pan and add the onion, carrot, celery and garlic. Fry over a medium heat for about 10 minutes until soft and beginning to colour.

2 Add the minced chicken and cook over a medium heat, stirring all the time to break up the lumps and seal the chicken. Don't try to brown it as you will get little hard pellets of chicken. Really work at breaking up the lumps.

3 Add the basil, thyme and marjoram, a generous grinding of pepper and some salt. Stir in the wine, tomatoes, sugar and chicken stock. Bring to the boil and then turn down the heat and simmer as slowly as possible for about 1 hour. You can half-cover the pan by sitting a wooden spoon across the pan and setting a lid on top. Check every so often to see that the sauce isn't sticking and reducing too much – add a little water if it looks too thick.

4 Cook the spaghetti according to the manufacturer's instructions; then drain, keeping back about 2 tablespoons of the cooking water. Return the spaghetti to the pan with the reserved cooking water and stir in the sauce (the water helps the sauce cling to the pasta). Serve piled into warmed bowls with loads of Parmesan and a pile of basil leaves.

# 35 Chicken Risotto with Herbs

| Quick and easy |
| --- |
| Preparation time 25 minutes |
| Serves 4 |

2 tablespoons olive oil

1 onion, finely chopped

1 garlic clove, finely chopped

400 g (14 oz) risotto rice

150 ml (¼ pint) dry white wine

about 1.2 litres (2 pints) hot chicken stock

350 g (12 oz) leftover cooked chicken, diced

50 g (2 oz) butter

4 tablespoons grated Parmesan cheese, plus extra to serve

1 teaspoon finely grated lemon rind

freshly ground sea salt and freshly ground black pepper

3–4 tablespoons mixed chopped fresh marjoram, parsley and lemon thyme

This is one of the best ways to use up leftover roast chicken – but the herbs must be fresh, it just will not work with dried herbs. I like to use a combination of marjoram, parsley and lemon thyme for their fresh, almost sweet flavours. Sometimes I lob in some frozen peas for a change and sometimes I cook shredded runner beans, toss them in olive oil and pile them on top – just don't forget the Parmesan! As always with risotto, use the best risotto rice – no other rice will do (my preference is for Vialone Nano, but Arborio is easier to find) – and Parmesan available (Parmigiano Reggiano is the one to look for – Grana Padano is a cheaper alternative). The stock, however, is just dandy made from a good-quality cube, but not too strong.

**1** Heat the olive oil in a large pan. Add the onion and garlic and stir-fry over a medium heat until the onion has become translucent. Add the rice and stir it around for a couple of minutes until it has become well coated in the oil and has turned translucent.

**2** Add the wine and boil rapidly for 1 minute, stirring, until almost evaporated. This boils off the alcohol, leaving the concentrated flavour of the wine in the rice. Now ladle in half the hot stock and bring up to the boil, stirring. Reduce the heat to a simmer and leave the risotto to cook until the stock has been absorbed.

**3** Add the rest of the stock and continue to cook, stirring regularly, until the rice is tender but with a little bite left in it and the texture is rich and creamy. This should take about 20 minutes in all.

**4** Stir in the chicken, butter, Parmesan, lemon rind, seasoning and most of the herbs and cook for a further 2 minutes. (You may have to add another ladle of stock; you're looking for a texture that is yielding but not stiff.) Then serve immediately, sprinkled with a little more Parmesan and a few more chopped herbs.

# 36 Risotto of Chicken Livers, Bacon and Chives

| |
|---|
| Informal supper |
| Preparation time 40 minutes |
| Serves 4 |

100 ml (3½ fl oz) olive oil

1 onion, finely diced

1–2 garlic cloves, crushed and diced

225 g (8 oz) arborio rice

150 ml (¼ pint) white wine

freshly ground sea salt and freshly ground black pepper

850 ml (1½ pints) Light Chicken Stock (see page 14)

4 smoked back or streaky bacon rashers, rinded

50 g (2 oz) butter

450 g (1 lb) fresh chicken livers, trimmed

50 g (2 oz) Parmesan cheese, grated

finely chopped fresh chives, plus a few long-cut chives to garnish

The creaminess of the livers, the saltiness of the bacon and the texture of the rice makes this one of my favourite dishes. It is a far cry from the standard liver, bacon and onions. I like to cook the bacon until it's crisp, giving a great contrast in texture to the whole dish. Serve just a big crisp green salad after this – it is very filling!

**1** The risotto base can be made up in advance. Heat all but a tablespoon of the olive oil in a large frying pan, add the onion and garlic and sweat over a medium heat for 6–8 minutes, until soft.

**2** Add the rice and stir well until it has absorbed the oil and become translucent. Add the wine and some pepper and cook over a medium heat for about 4 minutes, until the wine has evaporated.

**3** Pour in 750 ml (1¼ pints) of the stock and bring to the boil, stirring from time to time. Reduce the heat to a simmer and cook for 10 minutes, stirring occasionally.

**4** Now pour the contents of the pan into a large sieve set over a bowl. This separates the rice from the cooking liquid. Reserve the cooking liquid. Quickly transfer the rice to a baking tray and rake flat. Leave the rice to cool, then put it into a plastic tub and refrigerate.

**5** Heat a frying pan until hot, add the remaining olive oil and fry the bacon over a medium heat until crisp. Remove and drain on kitchen paper.

**6** Add 20 g (¾ oz) of the butter to the pan and, when it is foaming, season the chicken livers and add them to the pan. Fry for about a minute on each side until well browned all over but still pink in the middle, then transfer to a dish and keep warm.

**7** Combine the rice, the remaining stock and the reserved cooking liquid in a pan. Bring them to a simmer and warm through for about 4 minutes. Mix in the remaining butter, then finely chop the bacon and add to the risotto. Mix in the Parmesan and chives. Check the seasoning, but go easy on the salt as the bacon and Parmesan are already quite salty. Now divide between bowls and place the chicken livers on top. Garnish with a few long-cut chives.

# 37 Chicken All Sorts

| Informal supper |
| --- |
| Preparation time 20 minutes |
| Serves 4 |

2 tablespoons sunflower oil

100 g (4 oz) lardons (*cubetti di pancetta*)

2 medium courgettes, sliced diagonally

140 g (5 oz) chestnut or other well-flavoured mushrooms

350 g (12 oz) leftover cooked chicken, shredded

2 tablespoons light soy sauce (preferably Japanese), plus extra to serve

a squeeze of lemon juice

freshly ground black pepper

a huge handful of chopped fresh herbs (parsley, basil, chives, marjoram)

FOR THE BASMATI RICE:

½ teaspoon sea salt

300 g (10 oz) basmati rice

This has become a standard weekday dish in our family since it was introduced by my mother-in-law, Gill. The basics are chicken and rice plus anything else that's lurking around – French beans, pak choi, spinach, spring onions, peppers. The world's your oyster here. It's really a type of stir-fry with perfectly cooked basmati rice mixed in at the end. I find the results of traditionally cooked basmati rice a little too sticky for my liking; my method for perfect basmati rice, on the other hand, guarantees perfect fluffy rice every time.

**1** Heat the oil in a large wok or frying pan over a high heat, add the lardons and cook for 2–3 minutes until beginning to brown. Then add the courgettes and cook for 2–3 minutes.

**2** Throw in the mushrooms and stir-fry for 2–3 minutes. Now add the chicken, toss for a minute and then splash in the soy sauce, lemon juice and black pepper and throw in the herbs. Toss around to heat through, then stir the rice in quickly. Serve immediately, with more soy sauce to season the dish.

**Perfect Basmati Rice**

Bring a large pan (with a tight-fitting lid) filled with water (the secret of no-stick rice is to have at least five times as much water as rice) to the boil and add the salt. Wash the rice under cold running water until the water runs clear. Throw the rice into the pan of boiling water. Bring back to a rolling boil and stir once. Boil for exactly 7 minutes and then drain the rice well. Return to the pan and slam on a lid. Place the pan in a warm, not hot, spot and leave to steam in its own heat undisturbed for another 10 minutes. Fork up and serve. Perfect fluffy rice!

# 38  Jambalaya

| |
|---|
| Informal supper |
| Preparation time 45 minutes |
| Serves 4 |

**2 tablespoons sunflower oil**

**450 g (1 lb) boneless, skinless chicken breasts, cubed**

**225 g (8 oz) lardons (*cubetti di pancetta*)**

**1 large onion, chopped**

**4 celery sticks, chopped**

**1 red pepper, halved, seeded and diced**

**3 garlic cloves, crushed**

**300 ml (½ pint) passata**

**1.2 litres (2 pints) Light Chicken Stock (see page 14 or you could use a chicken stock cube)**

**2 teaspoons mild chilli powder**

**1 teaspoon dried oregano**

**2 teaspoons chopped fresh thyme**

**2 bay leaves**

**freshly ground sea salt and freshly ground black pepper**

**400 g can chopped tomatoes**

**450 g (1 lb) long-grain (not basmati) rice**

**chopped fresh parsley, to serve**

This is one of those great 'family-style' dishes that can be made in advance, kept in the fridge and reheated later. The dish is started on top of the stove, then finished in the oven, where the tomatoes and chicken stock are absorbed into the rice, giving it a great red colour; this is, in fact, a Creole-style 'red' jambalaya.

**1** Preheat the oven to 190°C/375°F/Gas Mark 5. Heat the oil in a large sauté pan and add the chicken and lardons. Gently fry until browned all over, then remove to a plate with a slotted spoon and set aside. Add the onion, celery, pepper and garlic to the pan and fry for 5–6 minutes, until the pepper has softened a bit and the onion has become soft and translucent.

**2** Pour in the passata and bring to the boil. Cook for another 5 minutes or so until the tomato starts to smell slightly caramelized and changes colour to a dark red.

**3** Pour in half the stock, scraping the bottom of the pan to mix in any brown sticky bits and stirring to combine well. The liquid should be fairly thick. Add the chilli powder, oregano, thyme and bay leaves and season with salt and pepper. Stir in the tomatoes and bring to the boil.

**4** Now add the reserved chicken and lardons. Pour in the remaining stock, stir in the rice and bring to the boil again. Tip into an ovenproof baking dish, cover with foil and bake in the oven for 20–25 minutes, or until the rice has absorbed all the liquid and is cooked through. Roughly fork up, scatter with the parsley and serve.

# 39 Chicken Laksa

| Smart entertaining |
| --- |
| Preparation time 20 minutes, plus soaking time |
| Serves 4 |

6 dried red chillies (or fewer if you can't stand the heat!)

1 onion, finely chopped

a small piece of fresh root ginger, peeled and grated

3 tablespoons Thai fish sauce (*nam pla*)

finely grated rind of 1 lime

3 tablespoons cashew nuts

$\frac{1}{2}$ teaspoon ground turmeric

1 teaspoon ground coriander

4 tablespoons vegetable oil, plus extra for the noodles

475 ml (16 fl oz) Light Chicken Stock (see page 14)

750 ml (1$\frac{1}{4}$ pints) coconut milk from a can or carton

225 g (8 oz) dried flat rice noodles

400 g (14 oz) boneless, skinless chicken breasts, cut into thin strips

225 g (8 oz) beansprouts

sprigs of fresh coriander, to serve

Of all the dishes I tasted on my travels whilst in the merchant navy, this sticks in my mind the most. It would be different every time I had it, depending on the location and what was to hand. It was always singingly hot (in both senses), had the local noodles in it and was a rich and aromatic broth. There are all sorts of texture contrasts going on here between chicken, noodles and broth, but one thing I liked was adding the beansprouts just before the broth was poured over the noodles – so you got a really great crunch the first time you dug in!

1 Soak the chillies in warm water for 30 minutes. Drain them, cut them in half and remove the seeds. Put the chillies, onion, ginger, fish sauce, lime rind, cashew nuts, turmeric, ground coriander and half the vegetable oil into a food processor or blender and process to form a smooth paste.

2 Heat the remaining oil in a non-stick frying pan, add the paste and fry for 5 minutes, stirring all the time to prevent sticking. Add the stock and simmer for a further 5 minutes.

3 Pour in the coconut milk, stirring constantly to prevent curdling. Bring to the boil and simmer, uncovered, for about 5 minutes.

4 Meanwhile, cook the noodles in a separate pan of boiling water according to the manufacturer's instructions; drain and toss in a little oil. Set aside.

5 Stir the chicken into the soup. Simmer for a further 3–4 minutes until the chicken is cooked.

6 To serve, divide the noodles between four deep bowls. Add the beansprouts and ladle over the hot soup. Top with the coriander sprigs and serve immediately.

# 40 Chicken Biryani

| Prepare in advance |
| --- |
| Preparation time 1 hour |
| Serves 4 |

a large pinch of saffron strands

450 g (1 lb) Perfect Basmati Rice (see page 56)

**FOR THE GARNISHES:**

4 tablespoons sunflower oil

1 large onion, sliced

50 g (2 oz) slivered almonds or cashew nuts

75 g (3 oz) raisins

3 tablespoons chopped fresh coriander

**FOR THE CURRY:**

1 tablespoon sunflower oil

1 onion, chopped

2.5 cm (1 inch) piece of fresh root ginger, peeled and finely grated

2 garlic cloves, finely chopped

2 tablespoons mild Indian curry paste (choose your favourite)

4 boneless, skinless chicken breasts, cut into large chunks

200 g can chopped tomatoes

1 teaspoon treacle or dark muscovado sugar

300 ml (½ pint) chicken stock

4 tablespoons plain yoghurt

freshly ground sea salt and freshly ground black pepper

When I was a callow youth, out on the town in Glasgow, I was a big fan of this after six beers too many. Tasting the real McCoy, however, opened my eyes to how good Indian cooking can be. Traditionally it is made in two parts – rice and curry, layered up in a dish and baked. I have developed a version that can be cooked on top of the stove in two pans, then mixed together at the last moment. It still tastes pretty special, and is fairly quick and easy to prepare. If cooking for later, layer it up in a dish, cover and reheat in the microwave. Curry pastes are always better to use than dry curry powder – there are bags more fresh flavours in a paste, and it keeps for longer without losing its punch.

**1** First prepare the rice. Put the saffron in a cup and pour on 3 tablespoons boiling water – leave to soak for 10 minutes. Meanwhile, cook the basmati rice as described on page 56. Once you've drained the rice and returned it to the pan, drizzle with the soaked saffron and water but don't mix it. Slam on a lid and place in a warm, not hot, spot and leave to steam in its own heat undisturbed for another 10 minutes. Fork up and set aside – you'll have yellow and white fluffy rice!

**2** To make the garnishes, heat the sunflower oil in a frying pan or wok and fry the onion slices until really dark brown but not burnt – this can take about 5–6 minutes. Remove with a slotted spoon and drain on kitchen paper. In the same pan, add the almonds or cashew nuts and raisins and stir-fry for 2–3 minutes until the nuts look toasted and the raisins plump up. Remove and set aside.

**3** Now make the curry. Add 1 tablespoon sunflower oil to the pan, then the chopped onion, ginger and garlic. Fry for 2–3 minutes and then add the curry paste and fry for 3–4 minutes until you really smell the spices. Add the chicken chunks, stirring well to coat them with the onions and spices, and cook for 5 minutes. Add the tomatoes, treacle or sugar, and stock. Bring to the boil, turn the heat down and simmer uncovered for about 15 minutes or until the chicken is cooked through and the sauce well reduced. Stir in the yoghurt and reheat without boiling. Taste and season.

**4** Now toss the curry quickly with the rice and serve immediately, garnished with the coriander, fried onions, nuts and raisins.

# 41 My Basic Chicken Stir-fry

| Quick and easy |
| --- |
| Preparation time 45 minutes |
| Serves 4 |

2 tablespoons groundnut oil

450 g (1 lb) boneless, skinless chicken breasts, cut into bite-sized pieces

450 g (1 lb) mushrooms (shiitake or chestnut), stems removed, thickly sliced

2 carrots, cut into matchsticks or thin diagonal 'coins'

1 small can whole water chestnuts, drained and sliced

1 small can bamboo shoots, drained

5 spring onions, shredded diagonally

1 tablespoon cornflour, dissolved in 2 tablespoons water

1 x quantity Perfect Basmati Rice (see page 56), to serve

**FOR THE STIR-FRY SAUCE:**

1 teaspoon sweet chilli sauce

2 garlic cloves, finely chopped

2.5 cm (1 inch) piece of fresh root ginger, peeled and finely chopped

3 tablespoons light soy sauce (preferably Japanese)

175 ml (6 fl oz) chicken stock (a cube will do!)

The secret of a good stir-fry is to have all the ingredients prepared well before you start to cook, as the cooking process only takes minutes. You should use a large wok, so that you can stir the ingredients around easily without them falling out of the pan! And don't be scared of the heat – get the wok very hot or you will end up with a stewed, soggy stir-fry. And it should have a lid – using one at the end helps to steam and cook the vegetables so that they are not completely raw. Feel free to change the vegetables – but cut them up very small so they cook quickly. This is one I make if it's been a long day!

**1** To make the stir-fry sauce, mix the chilli sauce, garlic, ginger, soy sauce and stock together in a small jug and set aside.

**2** Heat the groundnut oil in a wok until almost smoking hot. Add the chicken breasts and stir-fry for 5–6 minutes until lightly browned all over. Remove the chicken and put on a plate.

**3** Stir-fry the mushrooms, carrots, water chestnuts and bamboo shoots for about 3 minutes. Add the cooked chicken and the stir-fry sauce, stirring and lifting well to coat with the sauce. Cover the wok and cook very gently for about 3 minutes to reheat the chicken and finish cooking the vegetables in their own steam – this way you can be sure the vegetables are cooked.

**4** Lift off the lid and quickly stir in the cornflour and water mix. Bring to the boil to allow the cornflour to cook and thicken the sauce, stirring all the while so that it coats all the ingredients in the wok. Remove from the heat and divide between four serving plates. Garnish with the spring onions and serve immediately with the basmati rice.

# 42 Chicken Chow Mein

| |
|---|
| Informal supper |
| Preparation time 25 minutes |
| Serves 4 |

1 x 175 g (6 oz) boneless, skinless chicken breast

225 g (8 oz) medium dried egg noodles

3 teaspoons sesame oil

2 tablespoons sunflower oil

175 g (6 oz) fresh shiitake mushrooms, finely sliced

2 garlic cloves, finely chopped

50 g (2 oz) mangetout, finely shredded diagonally

50 g (2 oz) thinly sliced ham or pancetta, finely shredded into long strips

75 ml (2½ fl oz) chicken stock

1 tablespoon light soy sauce (preferably Japanese)

1 tablespoon mirin (Japanese rice wine) or dry sherry

freshly ground sea salt and freshly ground black pepper

6 spring onions, finely sliced diagonally

### FOR THE MARINADE:

2 teaspoons light soy sauce (prefereably Japanese)

2 teaspoons rice wine or dry sherry

3 teaspoons sesame oil

A great storecupboard staple, which makes a little chicken go a long way. It is cooked in three stages – the noodles are cooked first and then the chicken is stir-fried and then the vegetables, and finally the whole lot is tossed together. You can add other veggies, such as peas, sugarsnaps and so on, but don't add beansprouts until the very end or they will go soggy.

**1** Mix the marinade ingredients together in a medium-sized bowl with salt and pepper to taste. Slice the chicken into the thinnest, longest strips you can and mix with the marinade; cover and leave to marinate while you cook the noodles.

**2** Cook the noodles according to the manufacturer's instructions. When cooked, plunge them in cold water to stop them cooking, then drain and toss with 2 teaspoons of the sesame oil and set aside.

**3** Heat a wok over a high heat. Add 1 tablespoon of the sunflower oil and, when it is very hot and beginning to smoke, add the marinated chicken strips. Stir-fry quickly over a high heat for about 2 minutes and then transfer to a plate. Wipe out the wok with kitchen paper.

**4** Reheat the wok until it is very hot and then add the remaining sunflower oil. When the oil is hot and beginning to smoke, add the mushrooms, garlic, mangetout and ham or pancetta, and stir-fry for about 1 minute.

**5** Add the noodles, stock, soy sauce, rice wine or dry sherry, a little salt and pepper and the spring onions. Stir-fry for 2 minutes.

**6** Add the cooked chicken and its juices to the noodles. Stir-fry for approximately 3–4 minutes or until heated through and cooked.

**7** Stir in the remaining sesame oil and pile into warmed bowls – or carry the wok to the table and serve from there.

# 43 Velvet Chicken with Cashew Nuts and Yellow Bean Sauce

| |
|---|
| Quick and easy |
| Preparation time 10 minutes, plus marinating time |
| Serves 4 |

1 egg white

½ teaspoon salt

2 teaspoons cornflour

450 g (1 lb) boneless, skinless chicken breasts, cut into 2 cm (¾ inch) cubes

300 ml (½ pint) groundnut oil

75 g (3 oz) cashew nuts

1 tablespoon mirin (Japanese rice wine) or dry sherry

1 tablespoon light soy sauce (preferably Japanese)

125 ml (4 fl oz) yellow bean sauce

Perfect Basmati Rice (see page 56) or noodles, to serve

finely shredded spring onions, to garnish

I love contrasts of textures in a dish – something I seem to have in common with the Chinese! In this dish you have the soft, tender chicken contrasting with the crunch of the cashew nuts. The technique of 'velveting' the chicken in hot oil seals in the juices; then it is stir-fried with a spicy sauce and toasted cashews to add flavour and texture. Don't be afraid of the amount of oil used here – it's only for frying the chicken and is thrown away afterwards.

1 Lightly whisk the egg white, salt and cornflour. Add the chicken cubes, mix well, cover and chill for at least 20 minutes.

2 Heat all but 2 tablespoons of the groundnut oil in a wok or large frying pan until very hot. Have a colander placed over a clean dry bowl at your side. Carefully drop the chicken cubes into the oil, stirring and scooping to prevent them from sticking. After about 2 minutes when the cubes turn white all over and are no longer pink, tip the whole lot into the colander to drain.

3 Wipe out the wok with kitchen paper and heat it again until it is smoking. Swirl the remaining 2 tablespoons oil around the wok, then add the cashew nuts and stir-fry them for 1 minute. Add the rice wine or dry sherry, soy sauce, yellow bean sauce and chicken to the wok and stir-fry the mixture for another 2 minutes. Serve at once with basmati rice or noodles, garnished with the spring onions.

# 44 Paella

| Informal supper |
| --- |
| Preparation time 35 minutes |
| Serves 6 |

450 g (1 lb) mussels

175 ml (6 fl oz) dry white wine

6 tablespoons good olive oil

8 x 175–200 g (6–7 oz) chicken thighs

175 g (6 oz) chorizo sausage, cut into chunks

2 garlic cloves, finely chopped

1 large Spanish onion, finely chopped

1 large red pepper, halved, seeded and diced

450 g (1 lb) Spanish paella rice or Italian arborio rice

a good pinch of dried red chilli flakes

2 teaspoons sweet paprika

about 1.2 litres (2 pints) Light Chicken Stock (see page 14)

a large pinch of saffron strands, soaked in 3 tablespoons hot water

12 small ripe tomatoes, halved

100 g (4 oz) fresh or frozen peas

12 large raw prawns, in their shells

4 tablespoons chopped fresh flatleaf parsley

freshly ground sea salt and freshly ground black pepper

lemon wedges, to serve

A really good dish to make for a family feast in the summer. It has all my favourite things in it – chicken thighs, chorizo and mussels. Try to use saffron in the recipe – there really is no substitute. In Spain, paella is cooked by the father of the family, outdoors on a wood fire in a huge double-handled paella pan. They even make big gas-burners like huge picnic stoves so that you can cook it anywhere, as long as it is outside! Well, maybe our weather isn't really up to it, so give it a go inside and wash down with plenty of Rioja!

1 Scrub the mussels well, scrape off any barnacles and remove the beards that protrude from between the two halves of the shell. Discard any that do not close when lightly tapped on the work surface.

2 Choose a pan with a tight-fitting lid. Heat it dry and then put the mussels in. Add the wine, place the lid on and cook until the mussels open (this takes about 5 minutes). Do not overcook and discard any mussels that don't open in this time. Drain in a colander set over a bowl, cool and reserve both mussels and cooking liquid.

3 Heat the olive oil in a paella pan or large, deep frying pan. Add the chicken thighs and chorizo and brown all over, turning frequently. Stir in the garlic, onion and pepper and cook for about 5 minutes until softened. Stir in the rice until all the grains are nicely coated and glossy. Now add the chilli flakes, paprika, reserved mussel cooking liquid, stock and soaked saffron. Stir well, bring to the boil and simmer gently for 10 minutes.

4 Stir in the tomatoes, peas and prawns and continue to cook gently for another 10 minutes.

5 Once almost all the liquid is absorbed and the rice is tender, scatter the mussels on top to heat through for 2–3 minutes. Season to taste – you may not need very much salt as the chorizo and mussels are quite salty. Scatter over the chopped parsley and serve immediately straight from the pan, with lemon wedges to squeeze over.

# 45 Chicken, Broccoli, Almond and Orange Stir-fry

| |
|---|
| Quick and easy |
| Preparation time 15 minutes |
| Serves 4 |

3 large boneless, skinless chicken breasts

450 g (1 lb) broccoli

4 spring onions

3 tablespoons groundnut oil

3 garlic cloves, finely chopped

2.5 cm (1 inch) piece of fresh root ginger, peeled and finely chopped

125 ml (4 fl oz) chicken stock (a cube will do)

75 g (3 oz) halved blanched almonds, toasted

1 x quantity Perfect Basmati Rice (see page 56)

**FOR THE STIR-FRY SAUCE:**

finely grated rind and juice of 1 orange

2 tablespoons light soy sauce (preferably Japanese)

2 teaspoons cornflour

1 tablespoon oyster sauce

1 teaspoon sesame oil

1 tablespoon sweet chilli sauce

Broccoli is so good for you, especially when properly stir-fried. Too often it's served with thick raw stems and soggy tops. To get around this you need to cut the florets into small, even pieces, cutting through the thick stems. The sauce has a slightly sweet-and-sour style to it and the almonds are there to add a nice crunch. This is a good way to get kids to eat their greens!

**1** Slice the chicken breasts across the grain of the meat into long, finger-thick strips. Cut the broccoli into florets. Cut off the stalks and slice them thinly on the diagonal. Halve the spring onions lengthways, then cut them diagonally into 5 cm (2 inch) lengths.

**2** To make the stir-fry sauce, whisk together the orange juice and rind, soy sauce, cornflour, oyster sauce, sesame oil and sweet chilli sauce and set aside.

**3** Heat a wok over a high heat until it begins to smoke. Pour in half the groundnut oil and swirl around to evenly coat the sides. Add half the chicken strips and stir-fry by lifting and tossing them for 3–4 minutes or until they are no longer pink inside. Remove to a plate and repeat with the remaining chicken, adding more oil if necessary.

**4** Add the remaining oil to the wok. Stir-fry the garlic and ginger for 10 seconds, or until you can smell them but before they brown too much. Add the broccoli and stir-fry for 1 minute. Now add the spring onions and stir-fry for 30 seconds. Pour in the stock, bring to the boil and then cover with a lid and steam for 2 minutes or until the broccoli is tender but still crisp.

**5** Uncover and add the chicken and any juices to the wok. Push the contents of the wok to one side. Pour the stir-fry sauce into the clear side of the wok and cook, stirring, for 1–2 minutes or until the sauce has thickened. Then flip the chicken and broccoli mixture back into the sauce from the side of the wok and stir until glazed and coated. Sprinkle with the almonds. Serve immediately, with plenty of basmati rice.

# 46 Stir-fried Chicken with Peas and Bacon

| Quick and easy |
| --- |
| Preparation time 25 minutes |
| Serves 4 |

2 x 130 g packets of lardons (*cubetti di pancetta*)

140 g (5 oz) large spring onions, sliced

1 garlic clove, chopped

4 large boneless, skinless chicken thighs, cut into 4–5 long, thick 'fingers'

200 ml (7 fl oz) chicken stock (a cube will do)

freshly ground sea salt and freshly ground black pepper

1 tablespoon roughly chopped fresh mint

225 g (8 oz) fresh or frozen peas

2 teaspoons cornflour, dissolved in 1 tablespoon water

2 Little Gem lettuces, finely shredded

2 tablespoons double cream (optional)

3 tablespoons chopped fresh parsley

50 g (2 oz) butter

freshly squeezed lemon juice

2 tablespoons chopped fresh chives, to garnish

new potatoes or mash, to serve

You could call this a sort of French stir-fry! I love the combination of sweet peas and lettuce with salty bacon – especially with chicken. This is my version of a French classic but cooked for less time, to keep the vibrant spring flavours.

**1** Heat a frying pan until quite hot and add the lardons. Turn down the heat and cook for 2–3 minutes, stirring, until the fat starts to run and the lardons begin to take on a bit of colour.

**2** Add the spring onions, garlic and chicken pieces and stir-fry for 2–3 minutes until the chicken no longer looks pink and the onions are softening. Pour in the stock, season and bring to the boil, then turn down the heat and simmer, uncovered, for 8 minutes.

**3** Next add the mint and peas and then stir in the cornflour and water mix. Bring to the boil and, once the sauce has thickened and gone glossy, stir in the lettuce, cream (if using) and parsley. Give the pan a good shake while the sauce comes to the boil again, and add the butter. Let this melt into the sauce, simmer for 2 minutes, then taste, season with salt and pepper, and add a squeeze or two of lemon juice to lift it. Garnish with the chopped chives and serve immediately with boiled new potatoes or mash.

# 47 Tea-smoked Chicken with Avocado Salsa

| |
|---|
| Smart entertaining |
| Preparation time 40 minutes, plus marinating time |
| Serves 4 |

**4 boneless chicken breasts**

**100 ml (3½ fl oz) mirin (Japanese rice wine) or dry sherry**

**1 tablespoon sugar**

**1 tablespoon salt**

**2 tablespoons finely chopped fresh root ginger**

**FOR THE SALSA:**

**1 ripe avocado**

**2 ripe plum tomatoes, skinned, seeded and diced**

**½ red onion, finely chopped**

**3 tablespoons chopped fresh coriander**

**2 teaspoons chopped Japanese pickled ginger**

**2 teaspoons Thai fish sauce (nam pla)**

**1 mild red chilli, seeded and chopped**

**juice and finely grated rind of ½ lime**

**freshly ground sea salt and freshly ground black pepper**

**FOR THE SMOKING MIX:**

**200 g (7 oz) long-grain rice**

**200 g (7 oz) caster sugar**

**100 g (4 oz) lapsang souchong tea**

Hot-smoke your own chicken quickly and easily with the delicate fragrance of tea in a wok or covered barbecue. The chicken is amazingly delicately flavoured and tender. There can be a lot of smoke created here if you don't seal the wok properly – if you don't have a mega kitchen extractor, just take it outside the back door! If tea-smoking seems a bit tricky for you, the salsa is equally good with a pan-fried chicken breast (see page 12).

**1** Lay the chicken breasts in a glass or stainless steel dish. Mix together the mirin or dry sherry, 100 ml (3½ fl oz) water, the sugar and salt until dissolved, then add the ginger. Pour this over the chicken, turning to coat, then cover and marinate for 1 hour in the fridge.

**2** To make the salsa, halve the avocado and remove the stone. Peel and chop into tiny dice. Add the tomatoes, onion, coriander, pickled ginger, Thai fish sauce, chilli, lime juice and rind, season with salt and pepper, and mix well. Set aside while you smoke the chicken.

**3** Lift the chicken out of the liquid, pat dry and place in the base of a wide bamboo steamer – with a lid – which will fit inside your wok.

**4** Mix the rice, sugar and tea together. Line a large wok with foil and add the smoking mix. Place the wok over a medium heat. When the mixture starts to smoulder, place the bamboo steamer on top. Seal the seam between the bamboo steamer and wok with clean, wet cloths, to stop smoke escaping from the sides. Put the lid on, turn the heat down low and leave to cook and smoke for 20 minutes.

**5** Turn the heat off and leave to smoke for another 15 minutes. I recommend taking the wok outside when you remove the lid, as there may be a lot of smoke. The chicken will be perfectly cooked and lightly scented with the smoke. Serve warm, with the salsa.

# 48 Chicken Saltimbocca

| Quick and easy |
| --- |
| Preparation time 15 minutes |
| Serves 4 |

**2 large boneless, skinless chicken breasts (about 450 g/1 lb)**

**freshly ground sea salt and freshly ground black pepper**

**6 slices of prosciutto or Parma ham, halved**

**12 large fresh sage leaves**

**seasoned flour, for dusting**

**1 tablespoon olive oil**

**50 g (2 oz) butter**

**lemon wedges, to serve**

Some chefs get really hot under the collar about using chicken instead of veal. The fact is that most Italian cooks use turkey, but I prefer the finer texture and flavour of chicken. Use good olive oil for this and you will have a dish made in heaven.

**1** Slice each chicken breast in half horizontally into two thinner escalopes. Cut each half in three equal pieces, diagonally across the grain, so you have 12 escalopes. Put each escalope between sheets of cling film and bat out thinly without tearing. Season each escalope with a little salt and pepper.

**2** Lay half a slice of ham on each escalope, put a sage leaf on top and secure these to the chicken by taking a large stitch in the centre, with a cocktail stick. The escalopes are not rolled up.

**3** Dust each escalope with flour on both sides. Heat the olive oil in a frying pan, add the butter and wait until foaming. Fry the escalopes four at a time over a high heat for 1½ minutes, sage-sides down, then flip them over and fry for another 30 seconds until golden brown and tender. Remove and keep warm while you cook the remainder. Garnish with the lemon wedges – the dish needs lots of juice – and serve piping hot.

# 49 Peppered Chicken with Whisky Sauce

| Quick and easy |
| --- |
| Preparation time 20 minutes |
| Serves 4 |

3 tablespoons black peppercorns

4 boneless, skinless chicken breasts

4 teaspoons Dijon mustard

freshly ground sea salt

25 g (1 oz) Clarified Butter (see page 18)

50 g (2 oz) butter

50 ml (2 fl oz) light malt whisky

4 tablespoons Light Chicken Stock (see page 14)

3 tablespoons double cream

**TO SERVE:**

1 bag herb salad

1 tablespoon olive oil

new potatoes

I thought that, if this works for steak, it should work just as well for chicken – and it does! This is a simple dish but a real masterpiece. The chicken breasts are carefully fried and then basted in buttery, peppery juices. A word of caution – there might be a few flames when you add the whisky, so make sure that the pan is well away from your kitchen curtains.

**1** Crush the peppercorns coarsely in a coffee grinder or pestle and mortar if you're feeling energetic. Tip the crushed peppercorns into a fine sieve and shake out all the powder. This is very important because the powder will make the chicken breasts far too spicy. Now spread the peppercorns over a small plate.

**2** Lightly score the former skin-sides of the chicken breasts with a very sharp knife just to rough them up and make the mustard and peppercorns stick. Smear both sides of the chicken breasts with the Dijon mustard and coat them in the crushed peppercorns. Only now season with salt, because salting first would prevent the pepper sticking to the flesh.

**3** Heat a large frying pan until medium hot. Add the clarified butter and then the chicken breasts, former skin-sides down, and fry gently, without poking them around, for 10 minutes, turning once. Do not move them around too much in the pan or the peppercorn crust will fall off – the aim is to produce a good crusty coating on each surface. Now add the butter to the pan and allow it to colour to nut brown, basting the chicken breasts with the buttery juices as you go. Transfer the chicken breasts to a baking tray and leave in a warm place to rest.

**4** Add the whisky to the pan and boil over a high heat for 1 minute – the alcohol must be boiled off. Add the stock, bring back to the boil, pour in the cream and stir. Scrape together any gooey bits from the bottom of the pan. When it boils, it's ready.

**5** Dress the salad with the olive oil. Pour any juices from the chicken back into the sauce and place a breast on each plate with a pile of new potatoes and some salad. Spoon the sauce over the chicken breasts and serve.

# 50 Supremes of Chicken, Pan-fried with Apples and Cider

| Quick and easy |
|---|
| Preparation time 25 minutes |
| Serves 4 |

2 Granny Smith apples

4 chicken breasts (supremes), each weighing 150–175 g (5–6 oz)

freshly ground sea salt and freshly ground black pepper

1 tablespoon sunflower oil

50 g (2 oz) butter

1 teaspoon icing sugar

300 ml (½ pint) dry cider

300 ml (½ pint) Light Chicken Stock (see page 14)

150 ml (¼ pint) double cream

2 tablespoons roughly chopped fresh parsley and a tiny bit of fresh tarragon

lemon juice

I love the combination of chicken, caramelized apples and creamy cider sauce, flecked with herbs. It's a real classic. The apples must be a rich golden brown on the outside while perfectly cooked inside. This dish can look quite dramatic with the contrast in colours, while the creamy sauce clings to the chicken.

1 Peel, core and quarter the apples. Season the chicken breasts with salt and pepper. Heat a large frying pan until it's nice and hot. Add the sunflower oil and half the butter to the hot pan. When the butter is foaming, add the chicken breasts and cook for 7–8 minutes on each side, until lightly coloured and just cooked through. Remove them from the pan and keep warm on a warmed plate.

2 Add the rest of the butter and the apples to the pan, then sprinkle over the icing sugar and gently fry the apples for 3–4 minutes, until browned and glazed. Remove the apples from the heat and keep warm with the chicken.

3 Now add the cider to the pan and reduce until it's almost disappeared. Add the stock and again reduce, this time by about two-thirds. Add the cream and bring the sauce back to the boil.

4 Return the chicken breasts, the apples and any juices they have released to the pan. Warm everything through for 2–3 minutes. Add a tablespoon of the chopped herbs and season the sauce with salt, pepper and lemon juice to taste. To serve, place a chicken breast on each plate, spoon over the apples and sauce and sprinkle with the remaining herbs.

Sautéed and pan-fried

# 51 Chicken with Morels and Madeira

| Informal supper |
| --- |
| Preparation time 35 minutes, plus soaking time |
| Serves 4 |

75 g (3 oz) dried morels or other dried mushrooms

50 g (2 oz) butter

4 chicken breasts

4 shallots, finely chopped

150 ml (¼ pint) sweet Madeira

300 ml (½ pint) Light Chicken Stock (see page 14)

300 ml (½ pint) double cream

freshly ground sea salt and freshly ground black pepper

2 tablespoons chopped fresh parsley, to garnish

noodles tossed in butter and parsley, to serve

Morels are those funny brown mushrooms with the pitted, almost honeycombed caps, gathered fresh in the spring. When wild mushrooms are plentiful, I make this dish a lot, with morels, chanterelles or whatever I can find. There are no complicated ingredients (you can buy dried wild mushrooms in supermarkets now) or techniques, just lots of reduction to concentrate the mushroom flavour. Madeira is one of those fortified wines that go so well with the earthiness of the morel.

1 Soak the dried morels in 150 ml (¼ pint) warm water for at least 30 minutes.

2 Heat the butter in a sauté pan until foaming. Add the chicken breasts, skin-sides down, and brown all over. Remove to a plate and add the shallots to the pan. Cook gently for 5 minutes until soft and golden, but not brown. Set aside while you clean the mushrooms.

3 Take the morels out of the soaking water (reserving the liquid) and rinse them well under cold running water. A lot of grit can collect in the indentations. Squeeze them and pat dry on kitchen paper, and halve or slice any that are very big. Strain the soaking liquid through a coffee filter to get rid of any grit and reserve. Add the morels to the pan containing the shallots and cook over a gentle heat for a minute or so. Add the Madeira and bring to the boil, boil hard until almost reduced to a couple of tablespoons, then add the stock and the reserved soaking liquor. Stir well, then add the chicken breasts, cover and simmer for 20 minutes until tender.

4 When perfectly cooked, remove the breasts from the pan and keep warm. Pour the cream into the pan, and season with a little salt and pepper. Bring to the boil and boil hard until reduced by half. Return the chicken to the pan, spoon over the sauce and garnish with the chopped parsley. Serve with noodles tossed in butter and parsley.

# 52 Chicken Burgers with Garlic, Rosemary and Rocket

| Prepare in advance |
| --- |
| Preparation time 45 minutes, plus chilling time |
| Serves 4 |

**4 fat garlic cloves, unpeeled**

**15 g (½ oz) dried porcini mushrooms**

**1 tablespoon olive oil, plus extra for brushing**

**1 red onion, very finely diced**

**1 tablespoon chopped fresh rosemary**

**350 g (12 oz) chicken thigh meat, coarsely minced**

**100 g (4 oz) lardons (*cubetti di pancetta*) or smoked dry-cure streaky bacon, finely minced**

**a splash of balsamic vinegar**

**freshly ground sea salt and freshly ground black pepper**

**TO SERVE:**

**4 ciabatta rolls**

**mustard mayonnaise (dijonnaise)**

**100 g (4 oz) rocket**

I have to say that the thought of a chicken burger usually fills me with dread, but when I came up with this punchy one full of Italian or Mediterranean flavours, I soon changed my mind! Not only does it taste fantastic but it contains less fat than a conventional burger. Making the burgers with chicken thighs really improves both texture and flavour.

**1** Put the garlic cloves and mushrooms in a small pan of cold water and bring slowly to the boil. Simmer for 20 minutes; then drain and cool. Squeeze the mushrooms dry and chop them finely. Squeeze the garlic flesh out of the skins and chop roughly.

**2** Heat the olive oil in a frying pan over a medium heat and add the onion, chopped cooked garlic and the mushrooms. Cook for 5 minutes until the onion is very soft and the garlic is beginning to brown. Add the rosemary. Tip out of the pan into a bowl to cool.

**3** Mix the minced chicken and lardons or bacon with a splash of balsamic vinegar. Work in the onion and mushroom mixture and then season well with salt and pepper. Divide into four and, wetting your hands, shape into burgers. Put on a tray, cover and chill.

**4** When ready to cook, remove the burgers from the fridge and allow to come to room temperature. Brush with olive oil and grill, griddle or barbecue for about 5 minutes per side, or until completely cooked through with no pinkness in the centre when cut open.

**5** Meanwhile, warm the ciabatta rolls in the oven. Then, halve them, spread the base of each with a little mustard mayonnaise, top with a burger and add a handful of rocket. Slam on the lid and tuck in!

# 53 Pan-fried Chicken with Aubergine, Tomato and Basil

| |
|---|
| Informal supper |
| Preparation time 50 minutes |
| Serves 4 |

**4 boneless chicken breasts, with skin left on**

**freshly ground sea salt and freshly ground black pepper**

**3 tablespoons olive oil**

**25 g (1 oz) butter**

**FOR THE AUBERGINE AND TOMATO SAUCE:**

**450 g (1 lb) aubergine**

**2 teaspoons fine sea salt**

**3 tablespoons olive oil**

**1 onion, finely chopped**

**2 garlic cloves, crushed**

**150 ml (¼ pint) red wine**

**400 g can chopped tomatoes**

**1 tablespoon finely chopped fresh basil, plus extra to garnish**

This is one of the simplest dishes to make, but undercooked aubergine is a sin – cook it until it melts into the sauce. Use good olive oil here as it will add to the flavour of the dish, and give a creaminess to the sauce. Stir in lots of chopped basil right at the end to capture the fresh flavour of the herb.

**1** For the sauce, quarter the aubergine lengthways and then cut into 2.5 cm (1 inch) cubes. Put the cubes in a colander or sieve set over a bowl and sprinkle over the salt. Leave for 20 minutes and then rinse thoroughly under cold running water. Pat dry with kitchen paper.

**2** Season the chicken breasts with salt and pepper. Heat a sauté pan until it's nice and hot. Add the olive oil and butter to the hot pan. When the butter is foaming, add the chicken breasts, skin-sides down, and brown all over. Remove them from the pan and keep warm on a warmed plate.

**3** To make the aubergine and tomato sauce, put the olive oil in the sauté pan and set over a high heat. Fry the aubergine for about 3 minutes until golden brown on all sides. Add the onion and garlic, reduce the heat slightly and fry until the onion has softened. Pour in the wine and tomatoes, bring to the boil, boil for 2 minutes then return the chicken breasts to the pan, cover and simmer for 20 minutes.

**4** Lift the chicken out and keep warm. Bring the sauce to the boil and then cook for 2–3 minutes until reduced and slightly thickened. Season well and then add the basil and warm through.

**5** Spoon the sauce on to four warmed plates and place a chicken breast on top of each, garnishing with some extra basil, then serve.

# 54 Southern-fried Chicken

| Informal supper |
| --- |
| Preparation time 30 minutes |
| Serves 4 |

**1.5 kg (3 lb 5 oz) free-range or organic chicken, jointed into eight pieces**

**freshly ground sea salt and freshly ground black pepper**

**100 g (4 oz) plain flour**

**about 250 ml (9 fl oz) sunflower oil or 250 g (9 oz) lard (If you must), for shallow-frying**

To make really good fried chicken, start with the best organic or free-range chicken you can buy and joint it – this dish relies on the flavour of the chicken and the crisp skin. The joints are seasoned and quickly tossed in flour. Now comes the tricky bit. The chicken is shallow-fried very slowly (a spatter guard is essential here if you don't want to be shot at by hot fat!), traditionally in pure lard, turning only twice, until golden brown and crisp. If the lard frightens you, use sunflower oil instead and you will have Northern-fried Chicken! I like this served with baked sweet potatoes.

**1** Rinse the chicken pieces and pat them dry. Season well with salt and pepper. Put the flour in a plastic bag and drop the chicken in, three pieces at a time, shaking until evenly coated. Put the pieces in a single layer on a tray when coated.

**2** In a large deep frying pan or sauté pan, heat the sunflower oil or lard over a high heat until it bubbles when a little flour is sprinkled in. Carefully add the chicken pieces and turn the heat down to medium. Fry for 7–10 minutes (without moving) or until the undersides of the pieces are really brown.

**3** Turn the pieces over and cook on the other sides for 7–10 minutes or until cooked through and evenly brown and crisp. Lift the chicken out of the pan, drain on kitchen paper and serve immediately.

# 55 Chicken Goujons with Green Mayonnaise

| Smart entertaining |
|---|
| Preparation time 25 minutes |
| Serves 4 |

450 g (1 lb) thick boneless, skinless chicken breasts

4 tablespoons seasoned flour

2 eggs, beaten

100 g (4 oz) Natural Dried Breadcrumbs (see below)

vegetable oil

freshly ground sea salt

lemon wedges

FOR THE GREEN MAYONNAISE:

fresh mixed herbs and picked watercress or spinach (140 g/5 oz in total)

300 ml (½ pint) mayonnaise

freshly ground sea salt and freshly ground black pepper

What a great dinner-party starter! I serve the hot goujons on a large platter with small bowls of green mayonnaise, so that everyone can help themselves with their fingers and dip in. This really brings people together and gets the chat flowing!

**1** Cut the chicken breasts across the grain diagonally into thick 'fingers'. Have three dishes ready, containing the seasoned flour, beaten egg and breadcrumbs. Toss the fingers in the seasoned flour and shake off the excess. Next, dip the chicken fingers in batches into the beaten egg, turning them around until well coated. Give them a bit of a shake and dunk them in the breadcrumbs, tossing them about until evenly coated. At this stage you can lay them on a tray (as long as they don't touch), cover them with cling film and refrigerate until you are ready to cook.

**2** To make the green mayonnaise, pick over the herbs and strip the leaves from the stalks – you should end up with about 75 g (3 oz). Wash and dry them well on kitchen paper. Dollop the mayonnaise into a liquidizer or food processor and add the herbs and the watercress or spinach. Blitz until smooth and creamy. Taste and season, then pour into a serving bowl.

**3** Before you cook the goujons, get everything organized. Line a large plate or tray with a wad of kitchen paper, have a slotted spoon handy and have your serving dish warming. Pour some vegetable oil into a wok (or large pan) so that it is one-third full, or use a deep-fat fryer, and heat the oil to 190°C/375°F (use a cooking thermometer if necessary).

**4** Fry a few goujons at a time for about 2 minutes, until crisp and golden. Drain each batch on the kitchen paper and sprinkle with sea salt. Keep warm in a low oven with the door slightly ajar (the goujons will go soggy if it's closed) while you cook them all. Once they're all done, squeeze the lemon wedges over and serve with the green mayonnaise for dipping and dunking.

### Natural Dried Breadcrumbs
Put slices of stale bread, crusts removed, in a food processor and whizz until you have fine crumbs. Spread out on a wide tray and leave in a warm place for 12 hours. Keep in an airtight container for up to 2 weeks, or in the freezer for up to 3 months.

# 56 Chicken Kiev

| |
|---|
| Informal supper |
| Preparation time 1 hour 10 minutes |
| Serves 4 |

**4 chicken supremes (boneless breasts with wing bones attached), skinned right up over the wing bone**

**4 tablespoons plain flour**

**2 eggs, beaten**

**140 g (5 oz) fine fresh white breadcrumbs**

**sunflower oil, for deep-frying**

**new potatoes and green beans, to serve**

**FOR THE GARLIC BUTTER:**

**100 g (4 oz) butter, softened**

**2 small garlic cloves, roughly chopped**

**3–4 tablespoons roughly chopped fresh parsley**

**juice and finely grated rind of 1 lemon**

**freshly ground sea salt and freshly ground black pepper**

Everyone loves this classic dish, and I don't know why it isn't made more often. Don't be put off by the deep-frying – done the right way, the breadcrumb coating is crisp, the chicken moist and tender and the butter garlicky and oozing. To stop the butter bursting through during cooking and make it easier to handle, I like to freeze it in cork shapes. The butter must be very well sealed in with lots of egg and crumbs because if there's just one little leak it splurges out into the fryer and makes a terrible spluttering noise, leaving an empty Kiev.

**1** To make the garlic butter, put the butter, garlic, parsley, lemon rind and juice into a food processor, with salt and pepper to taste, and blitz until smooth. Spoon 4 heaped tablespoons of this on to a small tray lined with cling film and leave to firm up a bit in the fridge for 10 minutes. After this time you can pat the pieces into smoother cork shapes, wrap each one in cling film and then freeze them.

**2** Take the chicken breasts and remove the long fillets on the undersides. Place the fillets between two sheets of cling film and gently bat them out to double the size with a rolling pin, keeping them perfectly intact.

**3** Make a 'pocket' in each of the breasts by making a horizontal cut along its thick side, being careful not to pierce through to the other side. Lay the breasts and fillets on a flat tray.

**4** Now get really organized. Put the flour, egg and breadcrumbs in three separate shallow dishes. Tuck a 'cork' of garlic butter into each pocket. Brush with the egg and lay the fillet on top pressing its edges to enclose the butter. Pull the outer flaps of the pocket over the fillet to cover. Dust the whole lot with flour, brush with more egg and roll in the breadcrumbs. Place the kievs on a cling filmed tray and put in the freezer for 30 minutes to firm up.

**5** Pour some sunflower oil into a wok (or large pan) so that it is one-third full, or use a deep-fat fryer, and heat the oil to around 160°C/325°F (use a cooking thermometer if necessary). Flour, egg and crumb the Kievs once more. Lower two of them into the oil and fry for exactly 8 minutes. Lift them out and drain on kitchen paper. Keep warm in a low oven, with the door ajar to stop them going soggy, while you cook the remaining two. Serve with boiled new potatoes and green beans.

# 57 Chicken with Butternut Squash and Bacon

| Informal supper |
|---|
| Preparation time 40 minutes |
| Serves 4 |

6 x 150–175 g (5–6 oz) boneless, skinless chicken thighs

1 medium butternut squash

2 tablespoons olive oil

175 g (6 oz) lardons (*cubetti di pancetta*)

1 garlic clove, crushed

75 ml (2½ fl oz) Light Chicken Stock (see page 14)

freshly ground sea salt and freshly ground black pepper

1 tablespoon chopped fresh sage

1 teaspoon chopped fresh rosemary

2 teaspoons chopped fresh thyme

1 tablespoon chopped fresh parsley

brown rice, to serve

Butternut squash is one of the tastiest squashes with its dense, sweet nutty flavour. While its sweetness makes it perfect for roasting, it's also dense enough to be braised without falling to bits.

**1** Cut the chicken thighs into quarters. Halve the butternut squash and scoop out the seeds, then peel with a potato peeler and cut into large, chunky cubes.

**2** Heat the olive oil in a sauté pan and add the lardons. Cook for about 5 minutes until the fat begins to run, then add the chicken pieces and stir-fry until browned all over. Now add the garlic and squash cubes and cook for a few minutes, stirring to coat the cubes with the juices in the pan. Add the stock, season with salt and pepper and slam on a lid. Cook over a very low heat for 25 minutes – the dish will cook in its own steam.

**3** Remove the lid and stir in the chopped herbs. Slam on the lid and leave for 5 minutes for the flavours to mingle. Then serve straight from the pan, with some brown rice.

# 58 Chicken Sautéed with Fennel

| Informal supper |
|---|
| Preparation time 45 minutes |
| Serves 4 |

2 tablespoons olive oil

4 boneless chicken breasts, with skin left on

1 onion, sliced

2 garlic cloves, finely chopped

2 fennel bulbs, halved, core removed and thinly sliced

2 teaspoons chopped fresh rosemary leaves

150 ml (¼ pint) dry cider

150 ml (¼ pint) Light Chicken Stock (see page 14)

freshly ground sea salt and freshly ground black pepper

2 tablespoons chopped flatleaf parsley

The delicate, slightly aniseed flavour of fennel is one of the best flavours to put with chicken. Fennel can be tough if not cooked for long enough, so slice it thinly and cook until it is meltingly soft. I sometimes add a slug of Pernod before the cider to emphasize the fennel. The cider and rosemary add a sweetness to the sauce and make it extra special. Add a good splash of double cream at the end and then lift the whole dish with a good grinding of black pepper.

**1** Heat the olive oil in a large sauté pan, add the chicken breasts, skin-sides down, and fry until brown. Remove from the pan to a plate.

**2** Add the onion and garlic and fry for 5 minutes until soft and golden. Then add the fennel and rosemary. Cook for another 5 minutes, until the fennel begins to soften.

**3** Add the cider, bring to the boil and boil hard until reduced by half. Pour in the stock, season, and then replace the chicken breasts, skin-sides up, and cover the pan. Simmer for 25 minutes or until the breasts are cooked.

**4** Lift the chicken out and reduce the sauce until it is syrupy. Stir in the parsley and pour the sauce over the chicken to serve.

# 59  Creamy Vinegar Chicken

| |
|---|
| Smart entertaining |
| Preparation time 45 minutes |
| Serves 4 |

25 g (1 oz) Clarified Butter
(see page 18)

1.5 kg (3 lb 5 oz) chicken,
jointed into 8 pieces

5 large garlic cloves, unpeeled

green beans tossed in olive oil
and lemon juice, and mashed
potatoes, to serve

### FOR THE SAUCE:

5 tablespoons white wine
vinegar

300 ml (½ pint) dry white wine

2 tablespoons brandy

2 teaspoons Dijon mustard

1 heaped teaspoon tomato
purée

300 ml (½ pint) double cream

freshly ground sea salt and
freshly ground black pepper

2 tomatoes, skinned and seeded

A friend who trained at Leith's School of Food and Wine raved about this dish, which she learned to cook there. It is based on a similar one developed by the legendary French chef Michel Guérard. This is one of those classic dishes that we tend to forget about; having made it again recently, I realize it is simply fantastic! It's rich and creamy, with a balanced acidity. The secret is in the reduction of the vinegar: if the acid in both the wine and the vinegar is not boiled off correctly, the sauce will be too sharp. The long cooking of the garlic makes it taste almost nutty.

1 Heat the butter in a large sauté pan and brown the chicken pieces really well all over – always skin-side first. Add the garlic and cover the pan. Turn down the heat and cook for 20 minutes or until the chicken is tender. Remove the chicken and keep warm. Pour off all the fat from the pan.

2 Now open all the windows! To make the sauce, add the vinegar to the pan, stirring well and scraping up any sediment from the bottom. Bring to a rolling boil and boil until the liquid is reduced to about 2 tablespoons, no more.

3 Add the wine, brandy, mustard and tomato purée, mix well and boil again for about 5 minutes to reduce to a really thick sauce.

4 In a small, heavy pan, boil the cream until reduced by half, stirring frequently to prevent burning. Remove from the heat and fit a small sieve over the pan. Push the thick garlic and vinegar sauce through this, pressing the garlic cloves well with the bowl of a ladle or a wooden spoon to extract the pulp.

5 Stir the sauce and season to taste with salt and pepper. Cut the tomato into thin strips or dice and stir into the sauce. Arrange the chicken on a hot serving dish and spoon over the sauce. Serve with green beans tossed in olive oil and lemon juice, and mashed potatoes.

# 60 Chicken Sautéed with Potato and Spinach

| Informal supper |
|---|
| Preparation time 45 minutes |
| Serves 4 |

**1 tablespoon olive oil, plus extra for drizzling**

**25 g (1 oz) butter**

**4 boneless chicken breasts, with skin left on**

**1 onion, chopped**

**2 large potatoes, peeled and cut into large chunks**

**300 ml (½ pint) chicken stock**

**200 g bag of baby spinach leaves**

**freshly ground sea salt and freshly ground black pepper**

This is probably the easiest recipe in the book – a whole meal in a pan! The chicken is browned before steaming in the pan with the potatoes, which will start to disintegrate and thicken the sauce. Stirring in the spinach at the end ensures it stays bright green and keeps in all the vitamins and minerals.

**1** Heat the olive oil in a sauté pan and add the butter. When foaming, add the chicken breasts, skin-sides down, and fry until nicely browned all over. Remove to a plate.

**2** Add the onion to the pan and fry until soft and golden. Then stir in the potatoes and coat with the onions, butter and oil. Cook for 5 minutes and then pour in the stock and return the chicken breasts and any collected juices to the pan. Season with salt and pepper to taste. Cover and simmer for 25 minutes or until both chicken and potatoes are cooked through.

**3** Gently stir in the spinach, pushing it into the potatoes. Cover the pan again and allow to sit for 5 minutes, to wilt the spinach. Drizzle with olive oil and serve immediately.

# 61 Paprika and Red Pepper Chicken

| Informal supper |
| --- |
| Preparation time 50 minutes |
| Serves 4 |

**8 chicken thighs or drumsticks**

**freshly ground sea salt and freshly ground black pepper**

**3 tablespoons plain flour**

**3 teaspoons sweet paprika**

**2 tablespoons sunflower oil**

**25 g (1 oz) butter**

**2 large onions, sliced**

**1 garlic clove, crushed**

**2 large red peppers, halved, seeded and cut into thin strips**

**1 teaspoon redcurrant jelly**

**200 g can chopped tomatoes**

**1 teaspoon tomato purée**

**½ teaspoon chopped fresh thyme leaves**

**600 ml (1 pint) Light Chicken Stock (see page 14)**

**350 g (12 oz) new potatoes, halved**

**TO SERVE:**

**4 tablespoons soured cream or crème fraîche**

**2 tablespoons chopped fresh chives**

This is one of the first things I ever cooked in my basement flat in Byres Road, Glasgow. Apart from spaghetti Bolognese and chilli con carne, it was the first dish I had made with any degree of success. Nostalgia aside, I've updated it to suit my changing tastes, but it's still a tasty staple that freezes very well. The better the paprika the better the dish, so either go to a reputable wholefood store or make friends with a Hungarian! This is great served with pasta.

1 Preheat the oven to 180°C/350°F/Gas Mark 4. Make deep slashes in the flesh of the chicken thighs or drumsticks, right to the bone. Season with salt and pepper. Put the flour and 2 teaspoons of the paprika into a plastic bag and add the chicken pieces a few at a time, shaking to coat them in the flour. Remove them to a plate.

2 Heat a large frying pan until medium hot. Add the sunflower oil and enough pieces of chicken just to cover the base of the pan – don't crowd it or the temperature will drop and the chicken will end up stewing. Fry over a medium heat, turning now and then, until golden brown. Season well and spoon into a casserole dish. Fry the remaining chicken in the same way.

3 Add the butter to the frying pan, together with the onions, garlic, red peppers and remaining paprika, and fry for about 5 minutes. Add the redcurrant jelly, chopped tomatoes and tomato purée and cook for 2 minutes. Now stir in the thyme and the stock. Season well and simmer for 5 minutes.

4 Pour the mixture over the chicken pieces and stir in the potatoes. Cover with a tight-fitting lid and bake for about 25–30 minutes, until the chicken and potatoes are tender.

5 Serve straight away in warmed bowls, topped with the soured cream or crème fraîche and chives.

# 62 Chicken Livers and Pancetta with Mash and Red Onion Gravy

| Smart entertaining |
|---|
| Preparation time 35 minutes |
| Serves 4 |

**FOR THE GRAVY:**

**4 teaspoons red wine vinegar**

**1 tablespoon redcurrant jelly**

**400 ml (14 fl oz) Light Chicken Stock (see page 14)**

**2 tablespoons Red Onion Marmalade (see below)**

**FOR THE MASH:**

**450 g (1 lb) floury potatoes, such as King Edwards, peeled and cut into chunks**

**40 g (1½ oz) butter**

**50 g (2 oz) Parmesan cheese, finely grated**

**1 tablespoon chopped fresh chives, plus a few long-cut chives to garnish**

**FOR THE LIVER AND BACON:**

**2 tablespoons olive oil**

**8 thinly cut rashers of pancetta (Italian cured bacon) or best streaky bacon**

**350 g (12 oz) fresh chicken livers, trimmed**

**freshly ground sea salt and freshly ground black pepper**

This is posh liver, bacon and onions. Each ingredient has been given a little extra to make an addictively tasty starter. The mash is rich and creamy, contrasting with the sweet, textured gravy and juicy pink livers.

**1** To make the gravy, put the vinegar and redcurrant jelly into a small pan and leave over a gentle heat until the jelly has melted. Raise the heat and boil until thick. Add the stock and boil until reduced by half. Stir in the red onion marmalade and boil until the gravy has reduced to 150 ml (¼ pint) and is thick. Season well and set aside.

**2** For the mash, cook the potatoes in boiling, salted water until tender. Drain well, return to the pan and mash with the butter until smooth. Stir in the Parmesan and chives. Season, then set aside and keep warm. The mash will keep for up to 1 hour.

**3** Heat a large frying pan until very hot, then add the olive oil and pancetta or bacon. Fry for 1–2 minutes on each side, until crisp and golden. Keep warm to one side. Season the chicken livers with salt and pepper. Reheat the frying pan until very hot, add the chicken livers (don't crowd the pan; cook the livers in batches if your frying pan is not very large) and cook for just 1 minute on each side. You want the outsides to become lightly browned but the insides to remain pink and juicy.

**4** To serve, pile the mash into the centres of four warmed plates. Spoon the chicken livers on top of the mash and then top with two pieces of crisp bacon. Spoon the red onion gravy around the outside and garnish with some long-cut chives.

**Red Onion Marmalade**

Add a little of this to a meat gravy to give it a rich onion flavour. It's also good with cold meats, game and bacon. Finely slice 1.5 kg (3 lb 5 oz) red onions. Heat 85 ml (3 fl oz) olive oil in a large saucepan over a medium heat, add the onions, stir well, then season. Cook slowly, uncovered, stirring occasionally, for 1–1¼ hours, until the onions are soft, thick and dark and the sugary juices are caramelized. Add 125 ml (4 fl oz) best-quality sherry vinegar or Cabernet Sauvignon vinegar, and 2 tablespoons crème de cassis. Cook for about 10 minutes, until all the vinegar has boiled off and the marmalade is glossy. Leave to cool, then store in a jar in the fridge. If you pour in a tablespoon of olive oil to seal the top, it should keep for 6–8 weeks. These quantities will make 500 g (1 lb 2 oz) marmalade.

# 63 Marjoram and Lemon Chicken Kebabs

| Low fat |
|---|
| Preparation time 30 minutes, plus marinating time |
| Serves 4 |

6 x 140–175 g (5–6 oz) bone-less, skinless chicken thighs

20 small cherry tomatoes

**FOR THE MARINADE:**

2 tablespoons chopped fresh marjoram

2 garlic cloves, crushed

juice and finely grated rind of 1 large lemon

3 tablespoons olive oil

**FOR THE PILAF:**

1 small onion, finely chopped

1–2 tablespoons olive oil

1 garlic clove, crushed

50 g (2 oz) sun-dried tomatoes in oil, drained and roughly chopped

300 g (10 oz) long-grain rice

300 ml (½ pint) passata

300 ml (½ pint) Light Chicken Stock (see page 14)

juice and finely grated rind of 1 small lemon

3 tablespoons finely shredded fresh basil

freshly ground sea salt and freshly ground black pepper

These are great cooked on the griddle or under the grill, but nothing beats the barbecue for me. I've used my favourite, chicken thighs, in this recipe – the acid in the lemon tends to dry out chicken breasts, whereas the meat on the thighs is more gelatinous and has bags more flavour. Marjoram and lemon are one of the best flavouring combinations for chicken. They add a herbal sweetness to the meat when it's marinated. I've thrown in a recipe for tomato, basil and lemon pilaf, which is the perfect accompaniment to these kebabs.

**1** Cut each chicken thigh into four pieces. Place in a bowl with all the marinade ingredients, cover and leave to marinate at room temperature for 2 hours or in the fridge overnight.

**2** Soak bamboo skewers, if using, for 30 minutes in cold water. If you are going to barbecue your kebabs, allow about 40 minutes for the coals to reach the right temperature. If you are grilling your kebabs, preheat your grill to medium high after you have threaded the skewers.

**3** For the pilaf, sauté the onion in the olive oil for 5 minutes until lightly browned. Add the garlic and fry for another minute. Stir in the sun-dried tomatoes and the rice and stir well so that all the grains of rice get nicely coated with the oil. Stir in the passata and stock, bring to the boil, cover and cook over a low heat for 20 minutes.

**4** Meanwhile, thread six pieces of chicken and five cherry tomatoes alternately on to four 25 cm (10 inch) metal or bamboo skewers.

**5** When the pilaf is halfway through cooking, cook the kebabs on the barbecue or under the grill for 6–8 minutes, turning now and then, until golden brown.

**6** Uncover the pilaf and fork in the lemon rind and juice and the basil, and season with salt and pepper to taste. Spoon the pilaf into the centres of four warmed plates and arrange the kebabs on top.

# 64 Salt and Pepper Chicken

| Quick and easy |
| --- |
| Preparation time 15 minutes |
| Serves 4 |

450 g (1 lb) boneless, skinless chicken breasts

1½ teaspoons freshly ground sea salt

1 teaspoon Sichuan peppercorns

1 teaspoon black peppercorns

vegetable oil, for deep-frying

2 tablespoons self-raising flour

fresh coriander sprigs, to garnish

**TO SERVE**

Perfect Basmati Rice (see page 56)

stir-fried vegetables

lemon wedges

Dry-frying salt and Sichuan peppercorns together produces a really wonderful aromatic flavour – the amount here (enough for about eight people) is about the minimum quantity it is practical to make, but it does keep well in a screw-topped jar for several weeks. The inspiration for this recipe comes from my original salt and pepper squid and I wondered whether it would work as well with chicken. It does, but the secret is in keeping the chicken strips nice and thin, cooking them quickly so they don't dry out, and not overcrowding the pan when frying. These are absolutely delicious served with basil mayonnaise.

**1** Cut the chicken breasts into long, little-finger-sized strips. Set aside.

**2** Heat a dry, heavy-based frying pan over a medium heat. Add the salt and stir it around for a couple of minutes until it begins to look a bit grey. Tip it into a bowl, reheat the pan and then add the Sichuan peppercorns and toss them around until they darken slightly and start to smell aromatic. Tip them into the salt. In a coffee grinder or a pestle and mortar, grind the salt and Sichuan peppercorns with the black peppercorns, until you have a fine powder.

**3** Pour some vegetable oil into a wok (or large pan) so that it is about one-third full, or use a deep-fat fryer, and heat the oil to 190°C/375°F (use a cooking thermometer if necessary).

**4** Mix half the salt and pepper powder with the flour, place it in a plastic bag and add the strips of chicken. Give the bag a good shake so that all the strips become evenly coated with the highly seasoned flour.

**5** Deep-fry 5–6 strips at a time in the hot oil for just about 1 minute, until golden but still tender. Lift out with a slotted spoon to drain on kitchen paper and keep warm in a low oven while you cook the remaining strips.

**6** Garnish with coriander sprigs and serve with basmati rice, your favourite stir-fried vegetables and lemon wedges.

# 65 Chicken Satay Kebabs with Spicy Peanut Sauce

| Prepare in advance |
| --- |
| Preparation time 20 minutes, plus marinating time |
| Serves 4 |

**6 large boneless, skinless chicken breasts**

**75g (3 oz) rice vermicelli**

**FOR THE MARINADE:**

**3 teaspoons mild chilli powder**

**1 tablespoon light soy sauce (preferably Japanese)**

**2 teaspoons light muscovado sugar**

**a good pinch of ground turmeric**

**50 ml (2 fl oz) canned coconut milk**

**1 tablespoon lime juice**

**FOR THE SPICY PEANUT SAUCE:**

**3 garlic cloves, crushed**

**3 shallots, chopped**

**1 long, thin red chilli, seeded and chopped**

**2 teaspoons paprika**

**1½ tablespoons sunflower oil**

**175 ml (6 fl oz) canned coconut milk**

**2 tablespoons crunchy peanut butter**

**1 tablespoon light muscovado sugar**

**freshly ground sea salt**

Satay skewers can be threaded well in advance and kept on a tray, covered in cling film, until ready for cooking. The first time I tasted satay was in the late 1970s, when I was in Singapore. I saw kids cooking it, holding the wooden skewers with their little toes over the hot coals. Having been brought up on good traditional Scottish fare, I remember thinking it was the most exotic and delicious thing ever – it kick-started my passion for food. This comes pretty close to the original flavour. Mild chilli powder is a great spice mix to have in the cupboard. It doesn't just contain ground chillies but also paprika, cumin, oregano and often garlic. It gives a chilli kick to this dish without the tears!

**1** Cut the chicken breasts into 2.5 cm (1 inch) chunks. For the marinade, put 2 teaspoons of the mild chilli powder in a bowl and mix with the remaining marinade ingredients. Stir in the chunks of chicken and leave to marinate at room temperature for 2 hours or for up to 24 hours in the fridge.

**2** Shortly before you cook the kebabs, soak bamboo skewers, if using, in cold water for 30 minutes. Meanwhile, make the spicy peanut sauce. Put the remaining teaspoon of mild chilli powder into a coffee grinder with the garlic, shallots, chopped chilli and paprika and whizz to a smooth paste. Heat the sunflower oil in a small pan, add the paste and cook over a medium heat for 3 minutes. Add the coconut milk, peanut butter, sugar, and salt to taste, bring up to a gentle simmer and simmer for 2 minutes. Leave to cool slightly.

**3** If you are going to barbecue your kebabs, allow 40 minutes for the coals to reach the right temperature. If you are grilling your kebabs, preheat your grill to medium high. Bring a large pan of lightly salted water to the boil. Thread the chicken chunks on to metal or bamboo skewers and cook for 8 minutes, turning now and then, until the chunks are lightly browned but still moist and juicy in the centre.

**4** Meanwhile, drop the rice vermicelli into the boiling water, take the pan off the heat and leave them to soak for 3 minutes. Drain them well and leave to cool slightly before serving.

**5** Spoon the warm peanut sauce into four ramekins and serve with the kebabs.

# 66 Chicken Teriyaki Sticks

| Prepare in advance |
|---|
| Preparation time 15 minutes, plus marinating time |
| Serves 4 |

**4 boneless, skinless chicken breasts**

**sunflower oil, for brushing**

**FOR THE MARINADE:**

**1 teaspoon caster sugar**

**1 tablespoon mirin (Japanese rice wine) or dry sherry**

**2 tablespoons light soy sauce (preferably Japanese)**

**1 tablespoon sunflower oil**

**1 teaspoon Dijon mustard**

**a squeeze of lime juice**

**2 tablespoons runny honey, warmed**

I make this Japanese classic using thin strips of chicken zigzagged on to skewers. This way the marinade really penetrates the flesh and the strips cook really quickly. Most recipes include honey in the marinade, which tends to make the kebabs burn before they are cooked. A flash of inspiration led me to try leaving the honey out of the marinade, reserving it to brush over the chicken once it was cooked, and – bingo! – trouble-free teriyaki ever since. Remember: soaking wooden skewers before grilling will prevent them catching fire on the barbecue.

1 Cut the chicken into long, thin strips, 2.5 cm (1 inch) wide and about 5 mm (1/4 inch) thick.

2 Mix all the marinade ingredients together, except for the honey, and toss the chicken strips in it. Cover and leave to marinate at room temperature or overnight in the fridge.

3 Soak eight bamboo skewers, if using, in cold water for at least 30 minutes.

4 If you are going to barbecue your kebabs, allow 40 minutes for the coals to reach the right temperature. If you are grilling your kebabs, preheat your grill or griddle to medium high. Thread the chicken on to metal or bamboo skewers in a zigzag fashion. Brush the kebabs with a little sunflower oil and griddle (or grill) for 2–3 minutes on each side. Lift them off the griddle as they are done and brush them with warm honey before serving.

# 67 Moroccan Chicken Kebabs with Dates and Bacon

| |
|---|
| Quick and easy |
| Preparation time 30 minutes, plus marinating time |
| Serves 4 |

4 boneless, skinless chicken breasts

5 tablespoons olive oil

1 tablespoon lemon juice

1 teaspoon soft brown sugar

4 teaspoons harissa paste

2 garlic cloves, crushed

freshly ground sea salt and freshly ground black pepper

12 fresh medjool dates

6 rashers of rindless streaky bacon, cut in half

12 no-need-to-soak dried apricots

## FOR THE SPICED COUSCOUS:

1 onion, finely chopped

1 large garlic clove, crushed

3 teaspoons Ras-El-Hanout

350 ml (12 fl oz) chicken stock

225 g (8 oz) couscous

6 spring onions, thinly sliced

2 long, thin red chillies, seeded and finely chopped

50 g (2 oz) pine nuts, toasted

juice and finely grated zest of 1 lemon

1½ tablespoons each of chopped fresh coriander and chopped fresh mint

Real Moroccan street food – perfect for a summer barbecue! Walking around the streets of any village or town in Morocco, you will find these cooking on charcoal braziers and you have to eat them even if you are not hungry because they smell so good! I like to use a traditional spice blend for couscous and tagines called Ras-El-Hanout, which is available in large supermarkets. Make these kebabs well in advance and leave to marinate in the fridge – make sure they are well covered unless you want your butter tasting of garlic!

**1** Cut the chicken into 4 cm (1½ inch) pieces. Place in a bowl with 2 tablespoons of the olive oil, the lemon juice, sugar, harissa paste and garlic, and season with a little salt and pepper. Toss together well, cover and leave to marinate at room temperature for 2 hours or up to 24 hours in the fridge – the longer the better.

**2** Soak bamboo skewers, if using, in cold water for 30 minutes. Make a slit in the side of each date and hook out the stone with the tip of a knife. Stretch each piece of bacon with the side of a kitchen knife and then wrap one around each date. Thread the pieces of chicken, bacon-wrapped dates and apricots alternately on to four metal or bamboo skewers and set to one side.

**3** If you are going to barbecue your kebabs, allow about 40 minutes for the coals to reach the right temperature. If you are grilling your kebabs, preheat your grill to medium high. Cook the kebabs for 10–12 minutes, turning them every now and then, until the bacon is crisp and the chicken is cooked through but still moist and juicy in the centre. Keep the kebabs warm.

**4** Next, prepare the couscous. Heat half of the remaining olive oil in a medium pan. Add the onion and cook until it is soft and lightly browned. Add the garlic and cook for 1 minute, then stir in the Ras-El-Hanout spice blend and fry for another minute. Add the stock and bring it to the boil. Pour in the couscous in a slow, steady stream, bring it up to the boil and stir it once more. Cover, take the pan off the heat and set aside for 5 minutes. Now uncover the pan and fork up the couscous into separate fluffy grains. Fork in the rest of the oil and the remaining couscous ingredients, and season to taste with salt and pepper.

**5** Spoon the couscous on to four warmed plates and rest a kebab alongside.

# 68 Sesame Chicken Kebabs

| Quick and easy |
| --- |
| Preparation time 15 minutes |
| Serves 6 |

50 g (2 oz) pancetta or dry-cured streaky bacon, diced

450 g (1 lb) boneless, skinless chicken breasts, roughly cubed

1 egg white

1 teaspoon salt

½ teaspoon sugar

1 teaspoon cornflour

2 teaspoons sesame oil

6 canned water chestnuts, drained and finely chopped

2 spring onions, finely chopped

sesame seeds

oil for deep-frying (optional)

light soy sauce (preferably Japanese) and sweet chilli sauce, for dipping

These moreish little kebabs are like a Chinese-style satay. I've based my recipe on the mixture for sesame prawn toasts – the dish everyone loves when cooked just right – crisp on the outside and soft in the middle! Mincing the chicken with bacon or pancetta gives it the fat it needs to keep it moist as it cooks under the protective crunchy sesame crust. The water chestnuts are there for added crunch, but you could add chopped peanuts instead. You can grill or deep-fry the kebabs, if you prefer.

**1** Soak 24 small bamboo skewers, if using, in cold water for 20 minutes. Put the pancetta or bacon and the chicken cubes into a food processor and blitz to a very smooth paste.

**2** In a small bowl, whisk the egg white with the salt, sugar, cornflour and sesame oil. Add these to the processor and blitz until you have a smooth, slightly rubbery mixture.

**3** Transfer to a bowl, and work in the water chestnuts and spring onions.

**4** Take 1 heaped tablespoon of the mixture at a time and squeeze it around one end of a bamboo or metal skewer, extending the kebab halfway down. Repeat until all the mixture is used up.

**5** Sprinkle the sesame seeds on a small flat tray and roll each kebab in the sesame seeds.

**6** If you are going to barbecue your kebabs, allow about 40 minutes for the coals to reach the right temperature. If you are grilling your kebabs, preheat your grill to medium high. Alternatively pour some oil into a wok (or large pan) so that it is about one-third full, or use a deep-fat fryer, and heat the oil to 180°C/350°F (use a cooking thermometer if necessary). Either grill or barbecue the kebabs for about 1½ minutes on each side until cooked through and golden, or carefully drop into the wok or deep-fat fryer and fry for 2 minutes until golden. Drain on kitchen paper and serve immediately with separate bowls of soy sauce and sweet chilli sauce for dipping.

# 69 Chicken Tikka with Mint and Coriander Chutney

| |
|---|
| Informal supper |
| Preparation 15 minutes, plus marinating time |
| Serves 6 as a starter |

450 g (1 lb) boneless, skinless chicken breasts

flatbreads and red onion, thinly sliced, then salted, to serve

**FOR THE TIKKA MARINADE:**

2.5 cm (½ inch) piece of fresh root ginger, peeled

1 garlic clove, roughly chopped

1 teaspoon ground cumin

1 red chilli, halved and seeded

¼ teaspoon mild chilli powder

50 ml (2 fl oz) low-fat yoghurt

1 tablespoon olive oil

1 drop each red and yellow food colouring (optional)

freshly ground sea salt

**FOR THE MINT AND CORIANDER CHUTNEY:**

½ teaspoon tamarind paste (or the juice of ½ lime)

25 g (1 oz) fresh coriander (including the stems)

25 g (1 oz) fresh mint, young stems and all

1 fresh green chilli, halved and seeded

1 teaspoon sugar

150 ml (¼ pint) thick low-fat yoghurt

Tikka simply means 'cut in bite-sized chunks'. Cut in this way, the chicken cooks in minutes. I like to serve the cubes heaped in a big pile, with warm soft flatbreads, such as naans or even pitta breads.

**1** Cut the chicken into 2 cm (¾ inch) cubes.

**2** Put all the marinade ingredients in a blender or mini food processor and blitz until smooth. Scrape out of the bowl and mix with the cubed chicken. Cover and marinate for 2 hours or more in the fridge.

**3** Soak 6 bamboo skewers, if using, in cold water for 20 minutes. Heat a ridged griddle pan or start the barbecue.

**4** Make the chutney. Mix the tamarind paste or lime juice with ½ teaspoon salt and 2 tablespoons cold water until dissolved. Pick over and wash the coriander and the mint. The softer stems have loads of flavour in them so include as many as you can. Put everything except the yoghurt into a blender or food processor and blitz until it forms a rough paste. You can use this almost like a pesto and smear it on to the breads before you add the kebabs, serving the yoghurt separately, or you can mix it into the yoghurt to give a refreshing sauce.

**5** Thread the chicken on to bamboo or metal skewers, packing the cubes closely together. If you are going to barbecue your kebabs, allow about 40 minutes for the coals to reach the right temperature. If you are grilling your kebabs, preheat your grill to medium high. Griddle or barbecue for about 6 minutes, turning frequently – this will stop them burning and ensure that they cook evenly. Serve in flatbreads with the mint and coriander chutney and lightly salted, thinly sliced red onion.

# 70 Whole Tandoori Chicken

| Informal supper |
| --- |
| Preparation time 1½ hours, plus marinating time |
| Serves 6 as a starter |

**1.5 kg (3 lb 5 oz) chicken**

**1 teaspoon hot chilli powder**

**1 teaspoon salt**

**freshly ground black pepper**

**2 tablespoons lemon juice**

**50 g (2 oz) Clarified Butter (see page 18) or melted butter**

**FOR THE TANDOORI MARINADE:**

**3 tablespoons yoghurt**

**4 garlic cloves**

**1 tablespoon dark muscovado sugar**

**5 cm (2 inch) piece of fresh root ginger, peeled and chopped**

**1 teaspoon cumin seeds, roughly crushed in a pestle and mortar**

**1 tablespoon coriander seeds, roughly crushed in a pestle and mortar**

**2 red chillies, seeded and roughly chopped**

**1 teaspoon garam masala**

**a few drops of red food colouring (if you must)**

I don't like the garish red colour of tandoori chicken, although it is authentic, but I love the way it is cooked – marinated and baked. Although it is difficult to replicate the heat of an Indian *tandoor* (clay oven), I have cooked this very successfully in a kettle barbecue. This method uses indirect heat that circulates around the chicken, keeping it incredibly moist. You get a passable result in a hot oven, but the flavour is better on the barbie. Take the chicken out of the fridge at least 20 minutes before cooking – it lessens the trauma caused by the sudden heat, and keeps the bird tender.

**1** Start the day before. Pull the skin off the chicken, gripping the bird with a clean damp cloth if it gets a bit slippery. Using a sharp knife, make deep slashes in the thighs and breast of the chicken. Mix the chilli powder, salt, pepper and lemon juice together and then rub this all over the chicken, making sure it penetrates all the slashes. Set aside to marinate for 20 minutes.

**2** Meanwhile, prepare the tandoori marinade. Put all the ingredients (including the food colouring, if using), into a food processor and blitz to a smooth purée. Put the chicken in a good-sized glass or stainless steel dish and spread the marinade mixture all over it and into the gashes. Cover the chicken and leave to marinate in the fridge overnight.

**3** Preheat the oven to 220°C/425°F/Gas Mark 7. While the oven is heating, take the chicken out of the fridge and allow it to come to room temperature. Stand the chicken on a rack sitting in a roasting tin, spoon over any remaining marinade and drizzle with 1 tablespoon of the clarified or melted butter.

**4** Roast the chicken for 1 hour or until the juices run clear when the thickest part of the thigh is pierced with a skewer. Baste frequently with the remaining clarified or melted butter and the pan drippings. Remove from the oven and allow to rest before carving.

# 71 Deep-fried Wontons with Red Pepper Coulis

Smart entertaining

Preparation time 1 hour

Serves 4

**450 g (1 lb) boneless, skinless chicken breasts, roughly cubed**

**100 g (4 oz) pancetta or smoked dry-cured bacon, roughly cubed**

**4 cm (1½ inch) piece of fresh root ginger, peeled and roughly chopped**

**1 garlic clove, crushed**

**a small handful of fresh coriander leaves, roughly chopped**

**1 egg white**

**freshly ground sea salt and freshly ground black pepper**

**24 rectangular wonton wrappers (freeze the rest of the packet for another time)**

**vegetable oil, for deep-frying**

**FOR THE RED PEPPER COULIS:**

**4 red peppers, halved and seeded**

**4 tablespoons extra virgin olive oil**

**4 garlic cloves, roughly chopped**

**4 shallots, diced**

**1 tablespoon paprika**

**1 fresh red chilli, seeded and finely chopped**

**2 tablespoons balsamic vinegar**

**a small bunch of chives, to garnish (optional)**

I keep wonton wrappers in the freezer, then defrost them to make instant ravioli wraps. I also love them filled and deep-fried. The beauty of these little Asian/Mediterranean parcels is that you can prepare them in the morning, put them on a tray and cover them with cling film, then fry them in the evening just before you want to eat them. They are good both hot and cold and stay crisp for ages.

**1** First, make the coulis (this can be prepared in advance and stored in a sealed jar in the fridge until required). Preheat the oven to 190°C/375°/Gas Mark 5. Arrange the peppers, skin-sides down, in a roasting pan and brush all over with 1 tablespoon of the olive oil, then divide the garlic equally amongst them. Roast for about 30 minutes, until the peppers start to collapse and blacken around the edges. Remove the peppers, place in a bowl, cover tightly with cling film and leave for 15 minutes. Then remove the skins, which should slip off quite easily. Place the peeled peppers in a food processor, with the garlic and any cooking juices.

**2** Sweat the shallots in 1 tablespoon of the olive oil until soft. Stir in the paprika and cook for 1–2 minutes, then transfer to the processor, along with the chilli, vinegar and the rest of the olive oil. Process to a purée and push through a sieve if you don't like a rough texture. Set aside.

**3** Put the chicken, pancetta or bacon, ginger, garlic, coriander, egg white and 1 teaspoon of salt in a food processor and whizz to a smooth purée. Season to taste.

**4** Separate the wonton wrappers and lay them on a work surface. Place a teaspoonful of the filling in the centre of each wrapper and brush the edges with water. Bring two opposite corners together over the filling and then bring up the other two corners, pinching them to form a little frilly bag.

**5** Pour some oil into a wok (or large pan) so that it is about one-third full, or use a deep-fat fryer, and heat the oil to 180°C/350°F (use a cooking thermometer if necessary). Deep-fry 5–6 wontons at a time for about 1 minute, until crisp and golden. Drain on kitchen paper and keep warm while you fry the others.

**6** Spoon the coulis into saucers and sprinkle with the chopped chives, if using. Pile the wontons onto a plate and serve.

Hot and spicy

101

# 72 Jamaican Jerk Chicken

| Informal supper |
| --- |
| Preparation 1 hour 5 minutes, plus marinating time |
| Serves 4 |

2 onions, roughly chopped

3 red chillies, seeded and roughly chopped

2 garlic cloves

4 cm (1½ inch) piece of fresh root ginger, peeled and roughly chopped

2 teaspoons fresh marjoram leaves or thyme

½ teaspoon ground allspice

125 ml (4 fl oz) cider vinegar

125 ml (4 fl oz) light soy sauce (preferably Japanese)

1 tablespoon honey

freshly ground sea salt and freshly ground black pepper

1.5 kg (3 lb 5 oz) chicken, quartered, or 4 chicken quarters

Perfect Basmati Rice (see page 56), to serve

There's no point in beating around the bush – Ainsley Harriott's jerk chicken is simply the best and I can do no better, so here it is! He says to use chicken on the bone for better flavour and I whole-heartedly agree. So, for economy buy a whole chicken and joint it (see pages 8–9).

**1** Place the onions, chillies, garlic, ginger and marjoram or thyme in a food processor and blitz until well blended. Add the allspice, vinegar, soy sauce and honey and whizz again until smooth. Add salt and pepper to taste.

**2** Deeply slash the chicken quarters and place them in a large shallow dish. Pour over the sauce and chill for 2–3 hours or overnight.

**3** Preheat the oven to 200°C/400°F/Gas Mark 6. Transfer the chicken quarters to a rack and sit it inside a roasting tin. Pour over any marinade from the dish and roast for 40–45 minutes, basting occasionally with the marinade juices in the roasting tin, until the chicken is cooked through and blackened. Serve with basmati rice.

# 73 Chicken Enchiladas and Guacamole

| Informal supper |
| --- |
| Preparation time 15 minutes |
| Serves 6 |

12 soft wheatflour tortillas

250 ml (9 fl oz) sunflower oil

850 ml (1½ pints) Roasted Tomato Sauce (see page 50)

2 large cooked chicken breasts, shredded into strips

225 g (8 oz) white cheese, such as feta or Wensleydale, crumbled

a small bowl of thinly sliced red or green chillies

2 onions, finely chopped

3 tablespoons chopped fresh coriander

crisp mixed salad leaves, to serve

**FOR THE GUACAMOLE:**

2 ripe avocados, halved, stoned and peeled

juice of 1–2 limes (depending on juiciness)

½ onion, grated, or 1 garlic clove creamed with a little salt

1 fresh green chilli, seeded and very finely chopped

2 tablespoons chopped fresh coriander, plus extra to serve

freshly ground sea salt and freshly ground black pepper

A dish for total self-indulgence – and pretty quick to make, too. It's a hands-on feast and a great way to use up leftover chicken. Needless to say the kids will love this one (minus the chillies), as they can get really messy as well as eating something that's vaguely good for them! The tortillas must be passed through hot oil as this helps them to seal and brings out the flavour.

1 To make the guacamole, put all the ingredients into a bowl and roughly mash with a fork. Cover and set aside.

2 Shallow-fry each tortilla in very hot sunflower oil for 30 seconds. This heats them and makes them easier to seal – don't get them brown or crisp. Drain on absorbent kitchen paper and stack up, wrapped in a clean tea towel to keep warm, until all the tortillas are fried.

3 Reheat the tomato sauce and keep warm. Put all the other ingredients into separate bowls and set on the table.

4 The idea is to help yourself and assemble your own enchilada. To assemble, take a tortilla, spread it with a couple of tablespoons of the sauce, scatter with some chicken, cheese, chilli, onion and coriander and roll up. Eat immediately, with more tomato sauce, the guacamole and a big green salad.

# 74 Mexican Chilli Chicken

| |
|---|
| Informal supper |
| Preparation time 35 minutes, plus marinating time |
| Serves 6 |

**8 x 175–200 g (6–7 oz) bone-less, skinless chicken thighs**

**2–3 tablespoons vegetable oil**

**6 tablespoons chilli paste (for a home-made version, see below)**

**3 tablespoons tomato purée**

**1 chicken stock cube, crumbled**

**25 g (1 oz) dark chocolate, roughly chopped**

**400 g can red kidney beans, drained**

**toasted sesame seeds and chopped fresh coriander, to garnish**

**FOR THE MARINADE:**

**2 tablespoons balsamic vinegar**

**3 garlic cloves, crushed**

**½ teaspoon sugar**

**freshly ground sea salt and freshly ground black pepper**

I've added a tiny bit of chocolate to the sauce – just as Mexicans do in *mole poblano*, their famous festival dish of turkey in a dark and spicy sauce. It doesn't give the sauce a chocolate taste, but it does lend it an incredible depth of flavour. This is my humble version, with added beans!

**1** Cut the chicken thighs into large chunks. Mix all the marinade ingredients together in a bowl and add the chicken chunks. Mix well, cover and leave to marinate for at least 2 hours.

**2** Heat 2 tablespoons of the vegetable oil in a casserole or heavy pan and fry the chicken chunks until nicely browned all over. Remove to a plate with a slotted spoon.

**3** Reheat the pan, adding a tablespoon more oil if necessary. Add the chilli paste and fry over a medium heat for about 5 minutes until it thickens, scraping and stirring so it doesn't stick – this releases the aromas and oils from the spices.

**4** Stir in the tomato purée, stock cube and chocolate. Add 450 ml (¾ pint) water and bring to the boil, stirring to dissolve the purée and chocolate. Simmer for 20 minutes, stirring every now and then to prevent the sauce sticking.

**5** Add the chicken and beans and simmer for another 15 minutes or until the chicken is cooked through and the sauce is nice and thick. Garnish with toasted sesame seeds and chopped coriander, and serve with boiled rice or tortilla chips.

## Chilli Paste

To make your own chilli paste, toast 3 tablespoons of sesame seeds in a small frying pan, until golden. Put them into a blender or food processor with 2 roasted red peppers, with black skin removed (see page 101), 1 large roughly chopped onion, 8 plain tortilla chips (buy a bag and keep the rest to serve with the chicken), 2 roughly chopped garlic cloves, 2–3 tablespoons of mild chilli powder (see page 92), a large pinch of ground cinnamon, 2 cloves, a small bunch of fresh coriander (stalks and all), 3 tablespoons of peanut butter, and 150 ml (¼ pint) water. Blitz until you have a smooth paste.

# 75 Green Thai Chicken Curry

Smart entertaining

Preparation time 30 minutes, plus marinating time

Serves 4

4 x 175–200 g (6–7 oz) boneless chicken thighs, with the skin left on

4 tablespoons sunflower oil

400 g can coconut milk

200 ml (7 fl oz) Light Chicken Stock (see page 14, or you could use a chicken stock cube)

4 teaspoons bought Thai green curry paste, or 6 tablespoons home-made (see below)

6 kaffir lime leaves (or the grated rind of 3 limes)

$\frac{1}{2}$ teaspoon salt

2 tablespoons Thai fish sauce (*nam pla*)

a squeeze of lime juice (optional)

2 tablespoons finely chopped fresh basil, plus extra to garnish

2 tablespoons finely chopped fresh coriander

TO SERVE:

lime wedges

Perfect Basmati Rice (see page 56)

This really is one of those spicy comforting dishes that lodges in your taste consciousness. For me, if I get a craving for this, nothing else will do and I have to make it. It's no hassle to make a big batch of the spice paste (see below) and freeze it in ice cube trays. To make the curry in advance, I only add half the paste at the outset, cook and cool. When reheating, I add the rest to really cause an explosion of flavours. Similarly, if using frozen cubes of paste, keep one cube to stir in just before serving to maintain the vivid green colour of the sauce. Don't be mean with the paste – Thai food is all about punch!

1 Cut each chicken thigh into four even-sized pieces. Heat a frying pan or wok and add the sunflower oil. Fry the chicken pieces on a high heat until golden all over. Then add the coconut milk, stock, curry paste, kaffir lime leaves (or lime rind) and salt. Bring to the boil and simmer for 10 minutes or until the chicken pieces are tender.

2 Stir well to prevent any ingredients sticking and remove the kaffir lime leaves. Stir in the fish sauce, taste, season and add, if necessary, a squeeze or two of lime juice. Stir in the basil and coriander.

3 Arrange on serving plates. Garnish with extra basil and serve with lime wedges and basmati rice.

## Thai Green Curry Paste

There's nothing quite like making your own curry paste. There may seem to be a lot of ingredients, but a food processor makes light work of them. Seed and chop 6 long green chillies. Roughly chop 2 stems of lemon grass and 50 g (2 oz) fresh coriander. Peel and chop 2.5 cm (1 inch) galangal or fresh root ginger and 2 shallots. Peel 3 garlic cloves. Put all these ingredients in a food processor, along with 1 teaspoon ground cumin, the finely grated rind and juice of a lime and 150 ml ($\frac{1}{4}$ pint) chicken stock, and blitz until smooth. These quantities make about 300 ml ($\frac{1}{2}$ pint) or 12 tablespoons of paste, so you'll have enough to make two batches of curry. Unfortunately it's not easy to process less than this, but don't worry if this is too much, as you can freeze it for another day.

# 76 Quick Chicken Curry

| |
|---|
| Informal supper |
| Preparation time 35 minutes |
| Serves 8 |

2 tablespoons vegetable oil

900 g (2 lb) boneless, skinless chicken breasts, cut into 3 cm (generous 1 inch) cubes

2 onions, roughly chopped

4 garlic cloves, crushed

1 tablespoon grated fresh root ginger

1 tablespoon plain flour

1 tablespoon ground turmeric

1 tablespoon garam masala

1 tablespoon ground cumin

1 teaspoon chilli powder

400 g can chopped tomatoes

400 g can coconut milk

450 ml (¾ pint) chicken stock, made with 1 stock cube

4 tablespoons mango chutney

250 g (9 oz) baby spinach leaves, stalks removed

200 g (7 oz) Greek-style yoghurt

freshly ground sea salt and freshly ground black pepper

boiled rice and naan bread, to serve

A chef called Ben, who used to work with my good friend Phil Vickery, created this fab curry. Phil is always accusing me of stealing his recipes. This time I've stolen one that he's stolen – does that count? I make this recipe from Phil's book, *Simply Food*, a lot. It really hits the spot when I'm in the mood for a quick curry fix.

**1** Heat 1 tablespoon of the vegetable oil in a large pan and add the chicken cubes. Quickly fry the cubes until lightly browned all over. Remove from the heat and drain on kitchen paper.

**2** Add the remaining oil to the pan, together with the onions, garlic and ginger, and cook gently for a few minutes until softened and golden brown. Add the flour and spices and cook for a few more minutes.

**3** Add the tomatoes and coconut milk and return the chicken cubes to the pan. Add just enough stock to cover them, scrape any bits from the bottom of the pan and stir well. Bring to the boil and then reduce the heat and simmer for 20 minutes, stirring occasionally.

**4** Lastly stir in the chutney and add the spinach. Cook for a couple of minutes until the spinach has just wilted, and then stir in the yoghurt and season with salt and pepper to taste. Serve with some boiled rice and naan bread. Delicious.

# 77  Malay Chicken Curry

| Informal supper |
| --- |
| Preparation time 40 minutes |
| Serves 6 |

5 tablespoons vegetable oil

3 tablespoons bought spice powder, or fresh (see below)

450 g (1 lb) boneless, skinless chicken breasts, cubed

450 g (1 lb) pumpkin or butternut squash, peeled and cut into chunks

300 g (10 oz) new potatoes, halved

1 medium aubergine, cubed

1 teaspoon sea salt

400 g can coconut milk

3 ripe tomatoes, quartered

chopped fresh coriander, to garnish

plain boiled rice, to serve

**FOR THE ONION PASTE:**

3 onions, chopped

4 garlic cloves, chopped

1 tablespoon chopped fresh root ginger

8 dried red chillies, soaked and chopped (this will make the curry quite hot, so feel free to add less)

1 teaspoon sweet paprika

2 tablespoons chopped or ground almonds

1/2 stem of lemon grass, chopped

Malay curries tend to have a lot of 'sweet' spices in them, such as cloves, nutmeg and cinnamon, which make a very fragrant mixture. Fennel seeds are often included, adding a pungent, very slightly aniseed note to the sauce. This recipe makes a very hot curry, so feel free to add as little or as much chilli as you desire! A Malay technique used here is puréeing the onions and then frying them to release the flavours – this also gives a better, smoother texture to the finished dish.

1 To make the onion paste, put all the ingredients into a food processor. Add about 3 tablespoons of the vegetable oil and blend to a paste. You may need to add 1–2 tablespoons water to loosen the mixture – don't worry if you add too much, as it will evaporate during cooking.

2 To make the curry, heat the rest of the oil in a large sauté pan. Add the onion paste and fry for about 5 minutes. Stir in the spice powder and then the chicken, pumpkin, potatoes and aubergines, and coat with the onion paste and spice powder. Fry until the onion paste begins to turn brown, then add the salt and 500 ml (18 fl oz) water. Bring to the boil and simmer uncovered for 20 minutes.

3 Stir in the coconut milk and tomatoes and simmer for another 15 minutes, until the sauce is thickened and the vegetables are very tender. Scatter the coriander over the curry and serve with plain boiled rice.

**Malay Spice Powder**

I am really into spice blends at the moment, and have come up with a Malay blend that is really fragrant and nothing like the powders you find ready-made – dry-roasting whole spices releases the oils and the flavours. Put 2 tablespoons of coriander seeds, 1 tablespoon of cumin seeds and 2 teaspoons of fennel seeds in a heavy frying pan with 6 black peppercorns, 6 cloves, a 5 cm (2 inch) cinnamon stick and 1/4 teaspoon of freshly grated nutmeg. Dry-roast over a medium heat until you can smell the aroma – don't let them change colour or the flavour will change too and become bitter. Tip the whole lot into an electric food grinder (if you use a coffee grinder for this, it will never be the same – it will become a spice grinder from that moment on!). Stir in 1 teaspoon of ground turmeric and the spice blend is ready to be used.

# 78  Hot, Sweet and Sour Chicken

| |
|---|
| Informal supper |
| Preparation time 20 minutes, plus marinating time |
| Serves 4 |

450 g (1 lb) boneless, skinless chicken breasts, cut into bite-sized cubes

2 tablespoons light soy sauce (preferably Japanese)

½ teaspoon salt

freshly ground black pepper

2 tablespoons cornflour, for coating

vegetable oil, for deep-frying

**FOR THE BATTER:**

250 g (9 oz) self-raising flour

300 ml (½ pint) lager

freshly ground sea salt and freshly ground black pepper

**TO SERVE:**

Perfect Basmati Rice
(see page 56)

stir-fried sugar-snap peas

320 g jar of hot and sour sauce, warmed, or 1 quantity of my home-made Hot, Sweet and Sour Sauce (see below)

With a light, crisp batter revealing tender chicken inside, and a glossy, well-balanced hot, sweet and sour sauce (you can buy excellent jarred versions of hot and sour sauce, or make mine – see below), this recipe is a far cry from the usual soggy Chinese carry-out! Cooked well, it is a real treat and not that difficult to achieve. You'll find no pineapple here – but use fresh if you have to.

**1** Toss the chicken cubes with the soy sauce, salt and pepper. Leave to marinate for about I hour.

**2** To make the batter, whisk the flour, lager and salt and pepper until smooth. Use immediately once made. Place the chicken cubes in a plastic bag with the corn-flour and give it a good shake to coat them evenly.

**3** Fill a wok (or large pan) one-third full with oil, or use a deep-fat fryer, and heat to 190°C/375°F (use a cooking thermometer if necessary). Dip a third of the chicken cubes quickly into the batter, coating them well but shaking off the excess, and drop them into the hot oil. Deep-fry for about 1 minute, stirring gently to keep the chunks separate. Drain on kitchen paper and repeat with the remaining chicken.

**4** Divide the fried chicken between four warmed serving bowls and spoon over the warm sauce. Serve with bowls of basmati rice and some stir-fried sugar-snap peas.

## Hot, Sweet and Sour Sauce

To make your own hot, sweet and sour sauce, whisk together 3 tablespoons rice wine vinegar or white wine vinegar, 2 tablespoons light soy sauce (preferably Japanese), 4 tablespoons chicken stock, 4 tablespoons orange juice, the juice of 1 lime, 2 tablespoons dry sherry, 1 teaspoon cornflour, 2 tablespoons tomato purée and 2 tablespoons soft brown sugar. Heat 1 tablespoon vegetable oil in a medium-sized pan and add 2 finely chopped garlic cloves, 1 cm (½ inch) piece of fresh root ginger, chopped, and 2 seeded and chopped red chillies. Cook for 1 minute until golden and then whisk the liquid sauce mixture again and pour into the pan. Bring to the boil, stirring occasionally, and simmer for 2 minutes. Add 1 very finely sliced carrot and 4 shredded spring onions to the sauce and simmer gently for 2–3 minutes, until the carrot is tender but still crisp (add extra stock or water if the sauce is too thick). Your sauce is now ready to use.

# 79 Spicy Barbecued Chicken Wings

| Informal supper |
| --- |
| Preparation time 35 minutes |
| Serves 4 |

**16 chicken wings, wing tips removed**

**1 teaspoon ground cumin**

**2 teaspoons ground coriander**

**juice and finely grated rind of 1 lemon**

**freshly ground sea salt and freshly ground black pepper**

**4 tablespoons roughly chopped fresh parsley or coriander**

**guacamole (see page 102) and sour cream, to serve**

**FOR THE BARBECUE GLAZE:**

**4 tablespoons tomato ketchup**

**2 tablespoons maple syrup or honey**

**1 tablespoon Worcestershire sauce**

**1 garlic clove, crushed**

**2 tablespoons lime juice**

**a good dash of Tabasco sauce (I like the jalapeño one)**

I like to rub a spice mix into blanched and cooled chicken wings and leave them to marinate for a while before finishing them off on the barbecue and glazing them. This means the chicken is cooked through completely, without the glaze burning. The thing is to keep them moving, so that they cook evenly and build up a good glaze. Make sure you have plenty of napkins to hand – these are definitely a cutlery-free eating experience!

**1** Soak 16 bamboo skewers, if using, in cold water for 20–25 minutes. Meanwhile, bring a large pan of boiling water to the boil and add the chicken wings. Simmer for 3 minutes, then drain and cool.

**2** Mix the spices with the lemon juice and rind and salt and pepper. Rub the chicken wings with the spice mix and leave to marinate for 20 minutes.

**3** Preheat the barbecue – allow about 40 minutes for the coals to reach the right temperature. Mix all the glaze ingredients together in a small pan, bring to the boil and simmer for 2 minutes.

**4** Thread the marinated wings two at a time on to double bamboo or metal skewers. Barbecue over a medium heat for 2–3 minutes, watching that the spices don't burn.

**5** Now brush the wings liberally with the glaze and continue to barbecue over a medium heat for another 6–10 minutes, turning them often so they don't catch and burn. Baste occasionally with more sauce until they are well browned, sticky and crisp. (Alternatively, grill the wings under a medium-hot grill or bake them in the oven at 200°C/400°F/Gas Mark 6 for 20 minutes.) When done, pile on to a serving dish and sprinkle with the parsley or coriander before serving. Serve with guacamole and sour cream.

# 80 My Perfect Roast Chicken Dinner

| Informal supper |
| --- |
| Preparation time 1 hour 40 minutes |
| Serves 4 |

1.3 kg (3 lb) free-range or organic chicken

freshly ground sea salt and freshly ground black pepper

a few sprigs of fresh thyme

1–2 bay leaves

olive oil

4 large floury potatoes

8 parsnips

vegetable oil, dripping or goose or duck fat

a glass of white wine

½ chicken stock cube, dissolved in 150 ml (¼ pint) boiling water

steamed broccoli, to serve

A perfect roast chicken is a splendid thing. After 20 years of professional cooking my philosophy is – buy good ingredients, cook them properly and don't muck about with too many extra flavours. In no dish is this more true than roast chicken. We love this so much in the Nairn household that we roast a chicken nearly every week.

1 Preheat the oven to 200°C/400°F/Gas Mark 6. Untruss the chicken and let it come to cool room temperature before cooking. Feel inside the cavity between the legs and pull out any large pieces of fat still clinging to the insides. Season the cavity with salt and pepper and tuck in the thyme and bay leaves. Rub the outside of the chicken all over with olive oil and season well with salt and pepper. Slash down through the skin between the legs and the main body of the bird so that the legs go floppy. This ensures even cooking. Sit the chicken in a roasting tin and pour in a bit more olive oil, but not too much. Roast on the middle shelf of the oven for 20 minutes.

2 Meanwhile, peel the potatoes and parboil them in a large pan of boiling salted water for 10–12 minutes if large, 8–10 if smaller. Peel and trim the parsnips and cut them in half or in long quarters if very large. Set aside. Drain the potatoes well, then use a fork to roughen the outside of each potato to ensure a crunchy crust.

3 Pour a thin layer of vegetable oil or melt a couple of large tablespoons of dripping or fat in another roasting tin on top of the stove until smoking hot. Carefully add the potatoes, turning them in the oil or fat to coat. Make sure the fat heats up again.

4 Open the oven door, remove the chicken and baste it with the juices in the tin. Add the parsnips to the tin, turning them in the pan juices. Return the tin to the oven and bung the potatoes on the highest shelf over the chicken. Roast for another 40 minutes, basting everything occasionally and turning the potatoes at least once during cooking. When everything is looking golden brown, pierce the chicken in the thickest part of a leg with a skewer or small sharp knife to see if it is cooked and the juices run clear. If so, remove the chicken from the tin and set it on a warm plate, covered loosely with a piece of foil, to rest for 10 minutes.

5 Tip the excess fat out of the pan, return the tin to the oven and let the parsnips crisp up for 10 minutes. Remove the parsnips and potatoes from the oven. Turn

the oven off. Lift the potatoes out of the tin with a slotted spoon into a warm serving dish and do likewise with the parsnips; keep it warm in the oven with the door propped open.

**6** Now make the gravy. Set the chicken roasting tin on the heat, and add the wine and stock. Bring to the boil and boil furiously for 2–3 minutes, scraping up all the sticky bits from the bottom of the tin. Taste and season very well. Tip any juices that have flowed out of the chicken into the gravy, then strain into a warm jug or gravy boat. Serve the chicken immediately, with the potatoes, parsnips and some steamed broccoli.

# 81  Herb-crusted Chicken Breasts

| Quick and easy |
| --- |
| Preparation time 25–30 minutes |
| Serves 4 |

**4 boneless, skinless chicken breasts**

**1 egg, beaten**

**freshly ground sea salt and freshly ground black pepper**

**FOR THE HERB CRUST:**

**50 g (2 oz) butter, melted**

**4 spring onions, finely shredded**

**6–8 slices of stale white bread, crusts cut off**

**4 tablespoons chopped fresh mixed herbs (e.g. parsley, marjoram, chives and/or thyme)**

This recipe is an easy way to perk up a chicken breast with a herby flavour. It looks really dramatic with its bright green, crunchy top. Make up the breasts in advance by whacking on the topping, then covering and chilling them until you're ready to bake. Try brioche crumbs for extra poshness.

**1** Preheat the oven to 200°C/400°F/Gas Mark 6.

**2** To make the herb crust, melt the butter in a small pan and add the spring onions. Cook for a minute and then set aside. Tear up the slices of bread and blitz in a food processor with the herbs until you have fine green breadcrumbs. Tip into a bowl and gradually stir in the spring onion butter, until the mixture looks lumpy.

**3** Brush each chicken breast with the beaten egg and press on a layer of the breadcrumb and herb mixture. Season with salt and pepper, then lay the chicken breasts on an oiled baking tray. Bake in the oven for 20 minutes, until the flesh is cooked through and the crust is golden and crisp.

# 82 Pesto Roast Chicken with Roast Tomato and Bean Stew

| Smart entertaining |
| Preparation time 1½ hours |
| Serves 6 |

**1.5 kg (3 lb 5 oz) free-range or organic chicken**

**4–6 tablespoons My Home-made Pesto (see page 47)**

**freshly ground sea salt and freshly ground black pepper**

**6 tablespoons olive oil**

**700 g (1 lb 9 oz) broad beans in the pod, to give about 350 g (12 oz) podded beans, or 350 g (12 oz) frozen broad beans**

**600 g (1 lb 5 oz) baby plum tomatoes (*pomodorini*)**

**2 sprigs of fresh thyme**

Pushing flavourings between the skin and breast of a chicken before roasting adds flavour and helps keep the breast moist. Make this with real fresh pesto for a really powerful basil flavour. Adding small ripe plum tomatoes to the roasting tin around the chicken concentrates their flavour and draws out the juices. Baby broad beans add the finishing spring touch, with a dash of green and their sweet young flavour. Serve with buttered pasta.

**1** Preheat the oven to 190°C/375°F/Gas Mark 5. Untruss the chicken and let it come to cool room temperature before cooking.

**2** With your fingers, loosen the skin around the neck area of the chicken, and slowly work your hands under the skin, loosening it from the breast all the way towards the thighs. Now take the pesto in your hand and smooth it all over the breast, right down to the thigh joints, to form an even layer under the skin. Pat the skin down again to remove any air pockets. Tuck the loose neck flap under the bird. Sit the chicken in a roomy roasting tin and season well with salt and pepper. Drizzle with 2 tablespoons of the olive oil and roast in the oven for about 40 minutes.

**3** Meanwhile, if using fresh beans, take them out of their furry pods. Blanch in boiling water for 1 minute. Drain and plunge into a bowl of cold water to cool them down quickly. Drain again and pop them out of their grey skins. (If using frozen beans, cook in boiling water for 2–3 minutes, then follow the instructions for the fresh ones.)

**4** After 40 minutes, remove the chicken from the oven and turn the heat up to 220°C/425°F/Gas Mark 7. Add the tomatoes and pour over the remaining oil. Mix the tomatoes around and season them. Tuck in the thyme and put the chicken and tomatoes back in the oven to roast for about 20 minutes or until the tomatoes have collapsed slightly and the skins are beginning to brown. Whip the tin out of the oven, pierce the chicken in the thickest part of a leg with a skewer or small sharp knife to see if it's cooked and the juices run clear, and lift it out on to a carving board. Cover and keep warm while you finish the stew.

**5** Mix the beans into the tomatoes and cooking juices. Pop the tin back in the oven for a few minutes, to heat up the beans. Season well and serve with the chicken.

# 83 Roast Chicken with Sage Butter, Bacon and Bread Sauce

| |
|---|
| Smart entertaining |
| Preparation time 1 hour 25 minutes |
| Serves 4 |

1.5 kg (3 lb 5 oz) free-range or organic chicken

50 g (2 oz) butter, softened

8 large fresh sage leaves, finely chopped

8 rashers of dry-cured streaky bacon or 8 slices of pancetta

1 teaspoon finely grated lemon rind

freshly ground sea salt and freshly ground black pepper

crisp roast potatoes and steamed green vegetables, to serve

**FOR THE BREAD SAUCE:**

300 ml (½ pint) milk

2 blades of mace (optional)

1 bay leaf

2 sprigs of fresh thyme

a few black peppercorns

1 garlic clove, crushed

1 small onion, peeled and halved

2 cloves

about 75 g (3 oz) fresh breadcrumbs

50 g (2 oz) butter

2 tablespoons double cream (for ultimate luxury)

Sage is a really underused herb and goes perfectly with chicken. In fact, I sometimes serve this with a pile of deep-fried, crisp sage leaves. Bread sauce is sometimes seen as unfashionable but, properly made, it can be a joy with its silky texture and perfume from the herbs and onion. Perfect for dunking buttery, sagey chicken into!

**1** Preheat the oven to 190°C/375°F/Gas Mark 5. Untruss the chicken and slash through the skin joining the legs to the breasts. Let them flop open to ensure even cooking. Allow the chicken to reach cool room temperature before cooking.

**2** Beat the butter in a bowl and stir in the sage. Finely chop 2 rashers of bacon or 2 slices of pancetta and beat into the butter, with the lemon rind, salt and pepper. Using your fingers, loosen the skin around the neck area of the chicken and slowly work your hands under the skin, loosening it from the breast all the way towards the thighs. Take the sage butter in your hand and smooth it all over the breast to form an even layer under the skin. Pat the skin down again to remove any air pockets. Tuck the loose neck flap under the bird. Sit the chicken in a roasting tin and season well. Drape the remaining bacon or pancetta over the breast and legs. Roast in the oven for about 40 minutes, basting every now and then with the pan juices.

**3** Meanwhile, start the bread sauce. Pour the milk into a pan and add the mace (if using), bay leaf, thyme, peppercorns and garlic. Stick a clove into each onion half. Add the onion to the milk, making sure the cloves are submerged, and slowly bring to the boil. Turn down the heat and simmer gently for 5 minutes, then remove from the heat and allow to stand and infuse for at least 30 minutes.

**4** After the chicken has been roasting for 40 minutes, remove the bacon or pancetta and keep warm. Turn the oven up to 200°C/400°F/Gas Mark 6, baste the chicken with the pan juices and return to the oven for another 20 minutes to brown and finish cooking and for the skin to get really crisp.

**5** Finish the sauce just before serving. Strain the infused milk into a clean pan, add the breadcrumbs and whisk over a medium heat for 2–3 minutes until thickened. Season to taste. Melt the butter and pour this over the surface of the sauce (this will prevent a skin forming while you keep it warm: just beat it into the sauce with the double cream when ready to serve).

# 84 Roast Chicken with Apricot and Mint Stuffing

| Smart entertaining |
| Preparation time 1 hour 35 minutes |
| Serves 6 |

**1.5 kg (3 lb 5 oz) free-range or organic chicken**

**4 tablespoons runny honey, warmed**

**1 teaspoon black peppercorns, coarsely crushed**

### FOR THE STUFFING:

**75 g (3 oz) dried apricots, roughly chopped**

**1 tablespoon fresh mint leaves**

**100–125 g (4–4½ oz) brioche, torn into chunks**

**50 g (2 oz) butter, melted**

**freshly ground sea salt and freshly ground black pepper**

### FOR THE SAUCE:

**450 ml (¾ pint) Light Chicken Stock (see page 14)**

**2 tablespoons apricot and apple concentrate (available from health-food shops)**

**40 g (1½ oz) butter**

**4 tablespoons double cream**

Since tasting Hillary Brown's stuffed guineafowl legs years ago at the legendary La Potinière restaurant in Gullane in East Lothian (now under new ownership), I have been roasting chickens using a version of her delicious stuffing as an under-skin stuffing. The butter-soaked brioche crumbs bathe the chicken breast while it's cooking, keeping it moist and tender. In turn, the mint offsets the sweetness of the apricots and honey.

**1** Preheat the oven to 190°C/375°F/Gas Mark 5. Untruss the chicken and let it come to cool room temperature before cooking.

**2** To make the stuffing, put the apricots into a food processor and blitz until finely chopped. Add the mint leaves, brioche and melted butter and blitz in pulses until well blended. Season with salt and pepper.

**3** Using your fingers, loosen the skin around the neck area of the chicken, and slowly work your hands under the skin, loosening it from the breast all the way towards the thighs. Now take the stuffing in your hand and smooth it all over the breast, right down to the thigh joints, to form an even layer under the skin. Pat the skin down again to remove any air pockets. Tuck the loose neck flap under the bird. Sit the chicken in a roasting tin and season well with salt and pepper. Roast in the oven for 45 minutes.

**4** Mix the honey and peppercorns together. Remove the roasting tin from the oven and spoon this glaze over the chicken. Return the tin to the oven and roast the bird for a further 20 minutes, basting occasionally until the skin is golden and the chicken cooked. To check, pierce the chicken in the thickest part of a leg with a skewer or small sharp knife. If the juices run clear it is cooked.

**5** Remove the chicken to a carving board, cover with foil and allow to rest while you make the sauce. Spoon off any fat from the juices in the roasting tin and add the stock and apricot and apple concentrate. Set over a medium heat and bring to the boil, scraping all the sticky bits off the bottom of the tin. Boil hard until reduced by half. Add the butter and cream and continue to reduce, whisking occasionally, until the sauce is slightly syrupy. Taste and adjust the seasoning. Strain into a warm jug and serve with the chicken.

# 85 Lemon and Garlic Roast Chicken

| |
|---|
| Informal supper |
| Preparation time 1 hour 10 minutes |
| Serves 4 |

**1.3 kg (3 lb) free-range or organic chicken**

**2 juicy unwaxed lemons**

**1 bulb of garlic**

**a handful of fresh flatleaf parsley, stalks and all**

**freshly ground sea salt and freshly ground black pepper**

**olive oil**

**150 ml (¼ pint) white wine**

**150 ml (¼ pint) chicken stock**

**new potatoes and greens, to serve**

If you *are* going to mess about with a roast chicken, this is my favourite way. Shoving sliced lemon, whole garlic cloves and herbs inside the cavity really does perfume the flesh. There's no harsh, oily flavour of garlic – just a gentle hint of nutty garlic and lemon that permeates all the way through the bird. It does wonders for the pan juices, too, which make a very tasty gravy.

**1** Preheat the oven to 200°C/400°F/Gas Mark 6. Untruss the chicken and let it come to cool room temperature before cooking.

**2** Cut 1 lemon into eight wedges and cut the bulb of garlic in half across its equator. Feel inside the chicken cavity between the legs and pull out any large pieces of fat still clinging to the inside. Stuff the cavity with the lemon wedges, garlic halves and parsley.

**3** Halve the other lemon and rub the halves all over the skin of the chicken, squeezing to release the juice. Season with salt and pepper. Slash down through the skin between the legs and the main body of the bird so that the legs go floppy. This ensures even cooking. Sit the chicken in a roasting tin and drizzle with olive oil. Roast on the middle shelf of the oven for 1 hour, basting every 20 minutes.

**4** Pierce the chicken in the thickest part of a leg with a skewer or small sharp knife to see if it is cooked and the juices run clear. If so, remove from the oven and leave it to rest in the tin in a warm place for 10 minutes. Then remove the chicken to a plate, pouring off the juices into a small glass. When the juices have settled, skim off any fat from the top and discard.

**5** Now make the gravy. Set the chicken roasting tin on the heat, and add the wine and stock. Bring to the boil and boil furiously for 2–3 minutes, scraping up all the sticky bits from the bottom of the tin. Taste and season very well. Tip the reserved chicken juices in the glass into the gravy, then strain into a warm jug or gravy boat.

**6** The chicken is now ready for carving. Serve the chicken with the gravy, new potatoes and your favourite greens.

# 86 Chicken Baked with Sun-blush Tomatoes and Goats' Cheese

| Quick and easy |
| --- |
| Preparation time 35 minutes |
| Serves 4 |

**olive oil, for brushing and drizzling**

**175 g (6 oz) mild goats' cheese**

**8 sun-blush tomatoes, roughly chopped**

**1 tablespoon chopped fresh basil or marjoram**

**freshly ground sea salt and freshly ground black pepper**

**4 chicken supremes (see recipe introduction)**

**juice of ½ lemon**

**roasted cherry tomatoes, to serve**

I had this idea many moons ago, when I was consultant to a large poultry producer, finding new flavours that would go with chicken. This experiment became a surprise hit – and one that eventually made it to the supermarket shelves. It is so simple. Chicken supremes are breast fillets with the wing bone still attached, available ready-prepared from larger supermarkets and good butcher's shops. Sun-blush tomatoes are not dried for as long as sun-dried tomatoes and are often called mi-cuit (literally half-cooked). They are softer and less chewy than the sun-dried variety and are available from larger supermarkets and delicatessens.

1 Preheat the oven to 200°C/400°F/Gas Mark 6. Cover a baking sheet with foil and brush lightly with oil.

2 Mash or chop the goats' cheese in a bowl and stir in the chopped sun-blush tomatoes, basil or marjoram, salt and pepper.

3 With a very sharp knife, make a deep slash through the skin and along the length of each supreme. Make a second slash across this. You now have a good pocket in which to place the goats' cheese and tomato stuffing.

4 Spoon the stuffing into the pockets and set the supremes on the baking sheet. Sprinkle the lemon juice liberally over the supremes, drizzle with olive oil and season well. Bake in the oven for 25 minutes, until the flesh is cooked through and the skin is golden brown.

5 Allow the supremes to rest in a warm place for 5 minutes before serving with roasted cherry tomatoes.

# 87 Filo-wrapped Chicken Breasts, Stuffed with Ricotta and Spinach

| |
|---|
| Smart entertaining |
| Preparation time 50 minutes |
| Serves 4 |

**4 boneless, skinless chicken breasts**

**200 g bag of baby spinach leaves**

**175 g (6 oz) ricotta cheese**

**2 tablespoons grated Parmesan cheese**

**1 teaspoon finely grated lemon rind**

**freshly ground sea salt, freshly ground black pepper and freshly ground nutmeg**

**8 sheets of filo pastry**

**melted butter or olive oil, for brushing**

**new potatoes and green vegetables, to serve**

This is my take on the Greek cheese and spinach dish *spanokopitta*. Filo has gone out of fashion somewhat but it's a quick and convenient way to wrap a piece of chicken in crunchy thin layers of pastry. To stop the spinach leaking and making everything soggy, squeeze it out very well after cooking. For a posh presentation, cut the parcels in half at an angle and place one half on top of the other to show off the golden pastry, white chicken and green spinach.

**1** Make a pocket in each chicken breast by cutting horizontally through the thickest side – but stop before you cut right through.

**2** Put the spinach in a large pan and cook for a couple of minutes over a high heat, stirring all the time until it wilts. Tip it out into a colander to cool. Squeeze out as much moisture as you can and then roughly chop the spinach.

**3** Put the ricotta into a bowl and beat until soft. Mix in the Parmesan, lemon rind and salt, pepper and nutmeg to taste. Add the spinach and mix in. Open up the pockets in the chicken breasts and use a quarter of the ricotta and spinach mixture to fill each pocket.

**4** Take two sheets of filo pastry and brush them with melted butter or oil, keeping the remaining sheets covered with cling film to stop them drying out. Place one sheet of the filo pastry on top of the other, butter-side up. Set a stuffed chicken breast on the filo, about one-third up from the short end. Flick the short end of the pastry up over the chicken, flip the long end inwards, then carefully roll the breast up the length of the pastry, tucking in the ends as you go. Repeat with the other chicken breasts. Transfer to a buttered or oiled oven tray and brush with more melted butter or oil. Cover with cling film and refrigerate until needed.

**5** Preheat the oven to 200°C/400°F/Gas Mark 6. Bring the chicken to room temperature before placing in the oven and baking for 25–30 minutes, until golden. Serve immediately with boiled new potatoes and green vegetables.

# 88  Gratin of Chicken Livers and Parma Ham

| Prepare in advance |
| --- |
| Preparation time 25 minutes |
| Serves 4 |

**125 ml (4 fl oz) olive oil, plus extra for oiling**

**freshly ground sea salt and freshly ground black pepper**

**juice and finely grated rind of 1 lemon**

**2 garlic cloves, very finely diced**

**2 tablespoons fresh flatleaf parsley, finely chopped, plus extra sprigs to garnish**

**350 g (12 oz) fresh chicken livers, trimmed**

**4 slices of Parma ham, cut into 5 mm (¼ inch) wide strips**

This couldn't be easier and relies on the big robust flavours of the chicken livers and the Parma ham. The ingredients have to be the freshest and best for this to work – so no frozen livers for this one. All the work is done in advance and you can even take it straight to the table in the cooking dishes. You could use any porcelain or oven-proof ceramic dish but I prefer my individual cast-iron dishes. They're about 13 cm (5 inch) in diameter, the perfect size for one serving, and will last a lifetime.

**1** Preheat the oven to 240°C/475°F/Gas Mark 9. Lightly oil four 13 cm (5 inch) gratin dishes and sprinkle with salt and pepper.

**2** In a small bowl, make a dressing by mixing together the olive oil, lemon juice and rind, garlic and parsley.

**3** Cut the chicken livers in half lengthways and divide between the gratin dishes. They should almost cover the bottoms. Remember to season them. Now whisk the dressing again and spoon it over the livers.

**4** Sit the gratin dishes on a baking sheet and put them at the top of the oven. They need 7–8 minutes. Once cooked, the livers should still be pink inside. You can give them another couple of minutes if you like but they'll be well done and grey. Remove from the oven and garnish with sprigs of parsley. Scatter the Parma ham over the top and serve. Be careful, as the dishes will be very hot.

# 89 Saffron and Ginger Chicken Cooked in a Clay Pot

| Informal supper |
| --- |
| Preparation time 2 hours |
| Serves 4 |

**1.5 kg (3 lb 5 oz) free-range or organic chicken**

**8–10 bay leaves**

**couscous and mixed salad leaves, to serve**

**FOR THE SAFFRON AND GINGER BUTTER:**

**100 g (4 oz) butter, softened**

**a large pinch of saffron strands, crumbled (or a sachet of powdered saffron)**

**1 cm (½ inch) piece of fresh root ginger, peeled and finely grated**

**freshly ground sea salt and freshly ground black pepper**

Cooking chicken in a clay pot (chicken brick) is amazing – it keeps the bird so moist and tender and full of flavour. It's a really ancient method of cooking still used by the Chinese and in Indian cooking (think of the *tandoor* oven). Not only can you cook a whole bird this way but you can also use the brick as a braising dish or casserole. It is porous and needs presoaking in cold water before you use it, then everything is bunged in and the lid put on. It goes into a cold oven and comes to temperature as the oven heats up. A word of warning: place the pot and lid on cork mats or folded tea cloths when they come out of the oven – meeting with a cold surface could crack the hot terracotta.

**1** Untruss the chicken and let it come to cool room temperature before cooking. Soak both halves of the chicken brick in cold water for 15 minutes.

**2** Meanwhile, make the saffron and ginger butter. Beat the butter in a small bowl and stir in the saffron, ginger and salt and pepper.

**3** Using your fingers, loosen the skin around the neck area, and slowly work your hands under the skin, loosening it from the breast all the way towards the thighs. Now take most of the saffron and ginger butter in your hand, keeping a little for the outside, and smear it all over the breast right down to the thigh joints, to form an even layer under the skin. Pat the skin down again to remove any air pockets. Tuck the loose neck flap under the chicken. Smear the remaining butter over the outside of the breast and season well with salt and pepper.

**4** Line the base of the chicken brick with the bay leaves and sit the chicken on top. Cover with the lid and place in the cold oven. Switch the oven on to 200°C/400°F/Gas Mark 6 and cook for 1¼–1½ hours.

**5** After 1 hour, check whether the chicken is almost done by piercing the thickest part of a leg with a skewer or small sharp knife, to see if it is cooked and the juices run clear (if still pink, cook for longer). If the chicken is almost done, return it to the oven without the lid for another 15–30 minutes to brown the breast a bit. Transfer to a board to carve and pour the cooking juices into a jug – they will be gingery and bay-scented. Serve with couscous and mixed salad leaves.

# 90 Poule au Pot with Stuffed Cabbage Leaves

| Informal supper |
| --- |
| Preparation time 2 hours |
| Serves 6 |

1.3 kg (3 lb) free-range or organic chicken

5 carrots, halved lengthways

3 celery hearts, quartered

3 large leeks, split, washed and roughly chopped

1 onion, stuck with a clove

1 bouquet garni

1 teaspoon sea salt

1 tablespoon black peppercorns

1 small dried bird's eye chilli

**FOR THE STUFFED CABBAGE LEAVES:**

2 tablespoons olive oil

1 onion, finely chopped

1 garlic clove, chopped

175 g (6 oz) stale breadcrumbs

140 g (5 oz) cooked smoked ham or gammon, finely diced

4 tablespoons mixed chopped fresh thyme, marjoram and parsley

juice and finely grated rind of ½ lemon

freshly ground sea salt and freshly ground black pepper

1 egg, beaten

6 medium Savoy cabbage leaves

This is a really easy one-pot meal to feed a large group of friends or family without any hassle at all. The French have been doing this with chicken and beef for centuries. Masses of vegetables and herbs are simmered with the chicken in a huge pot of water. This turns into a pot of delicious broth and a moist poached chicken. Sometimes a whole stuffed cabbage is added, but I prefer to add individual packets of stuffing so there's no need for potatoes. Try serving the broth as a soup to start off with, then tuck in!

1 Wash the chicken inside and out, and pull out any loose fat from the cavity. Put half the carrots, celery and leeks, and the onion, in the bottom of a very large deep pan. Sit the chicken on top and add the remaining carrots, celery and leeks, and the bouquet garni, salt, peppercorns and chilli. Pour in enough water just to cover (about 2.5 litres/4½ pints). Bring slowly to the boil, skimming off any grey scum that arises. Simmer very slowly – so that the broth remains clear – for 45 minutes, skimming occasionally.

2 Meanwhile, make the stuffed cabbage leaves. Heat the olive oil and add the onion and garlic. Cook for 5–6 minutes until soft and golden and tip into a mixing bowl to cool. Add the breadcrumbs, ham or gammon, herbs, lemon juice and rind, salt and pepper and the beaten egg and mix well.

3 Take a cabbage leaf and lay it stalk-side uppermost. Spoon one-sixth of the stuffing on to the centre and fold the two opposite edges inwards to enclose the stuffing, then the two remaining edges. Secure with a cocktail stick. Repeat with the remaining cabbage leaves and stuffing.

4 Carefully place the cabbage parcels in the pan on top of the chicken. Cover and simmer for a further 20 minutes.

5 To serve, lift the parcels out on to a plate. then lift out the chicken and place it on a large serving dish, surrounded by the cooked vegetables and the stuffed cabbage leaves. Spoon over a little broth and serve. If you like, cover the chicken and keep it warm while you serve the broth as a clear soup to start the meal.

# 91 Coq au Vin

| Smart entertaining |
| --- |
| Preparation time 1½ hours |
| Serves 4–6 |

1 bottle of light red wine

4 tablespoons brandy

2 bay leaves

2 bouquets garnis (tied bundles of dried bay, thyme and parsley stalks)

a few sprigs of fresh thyme

1 garlic clove, bruised

1.5 kg (3 lb 5 oz) free-range or organic chicken, jointed into 8 pieces

seasoned flour, for coating

125 g (4½ oz) butter

130 g packet of lardons (*cubetti di pancetta*)

300 ml (½ pint) Light Chicken Stock (see page 14)

225 g (8 oz) small pickling onions

225 g (8 oz) brown cap mushrooms

freshly ground sea salt and freshly ground black pepper

chopped fresh parsley, to serve

**FOR THE BEURRE MANIÉ:**

50 g (2 oz) butter, softened

2 tablespoons plain flour

For my version of this time-honoured classic I like to reduce the wine first to boil off the raw taste of the alcohol and concentrate the flavour. Don't be tempted to use a cheap wine that you wouldn't drink for this as it will taste dreadful! This dish used to be made with a tough old cockerel and was stewed for hours to tenderize it. We have to use what is available to us, so I really would use a free-range or organic chicken here, to give both flavour and texture to the dish.

1 Pour the wine and brandy into a pan and add the bay leaves, 1 bouquet garni, the thyme sprigs and the garlic. Bring to the boil and simmer until reduced by half. Allow to cool.

2 Toss the chicken pieces in a little seasoned flour. Melt half the butter in a large frying pan. When foaming, add the chicken pieces and brown them all over, then transfer them to a flameproof casserole. Add the lardons to the frying pan and fry until golden. Remove with a slotted spoon and add to the chicken.

3 Strain the cooled reduced wine mixture over the chicken and pour over the stock. Tuck in the remaining bouquet garni. Bring to the boil, then lower the heat, cover and simmer very slowly for 30 minutes. (If preferred, cook the casserole in the oven at 180°C/350°F/Gas Mark 4.)

4 Meanwhile, peel the onions and halve them, but leave the root ends intact to hold them together. Halve or quarter the mushrooms if large. Melt the remaining butter in a frying pan, add the onions and fry for about 5 minutes until tender and lightly browned. Add the mushrooms and fry until softened. Add the mushrooms and onions to the casserole, cover and cook for a further 10 minutes or until the chicken is tender.

5 For the beurre manié, work the butter and flour together with a wooden spoon to a smooth paste.

6 Lift out the chicken pieces and vegetables and place in a warm serving dish; cover and keep warm. Bring the cooking liquid in the casserole to the boil. Whisk in the beurre manié, a little at a time, until the sauce is shiny and syrupy. Add salt and pepper to taste. Pour the sauce over the chicken, scatter over the parsley and serve.

# 92 Garlic Chicken Stovies

Preparation time 1½ hours

Serves 4

75 g (3 oz) butter or duck or goose fat

1.5 kg (3 lb 5 oz) free-range or organic chicken, jointed into 8 pieces

2 large onions, thinly sliced

900 g (2 lb) floury potatoes, peeled and thickly sliced

3 tablespoons olive oil

8 fat garlic cloves, unpeeled

finely grated rind of 1 lemon

2 teaspoons chopped fresh thyme

2 teaspoons chopped fresh rosemary leaves

1 bay leaf

freshly ground sea salt and freshly ground black pepper

300 ml (½ pint) boiling Light Chicken Stock (see page 14)

steamed young kale and glazed carrots, to serve

Only floury potatoes work here – the sort that disintegrate when they cook – because you want them to break down and thicken the stew during cooking. I use King Edwards, Kerr's Pinks or Golden Wonder, but other suitable varieties such as Pentland, Maris Piper or Duke of York will do. The origin of the word 'stovies' is said to be a genuine old Scots term 'to stove', meaning to cook in an enclosed dish. Others say it comes from the French *étuver* – to stew. Wherever the name comes from, everyone in Scotland has their own way of making 'stovies' – usually involving onions cooked in dripping, potatoes and the leftover cold roast from a Sunday meal. This is Maxine Clark's posh version with a French accent!

1 Preheat the oven to 180°C/350°F/Gas Mark 5. Melt 50 g (2 oz) of the butter or fat until foaming in a frying pan and brown the chicken joints evenly all over. Remove to a plate with a slotted spoon and add the onions. Cook these over a medium heat for about 10 minutes until really soft and golden and just beginning to brown.

2 Toss the potatoes with the olive oil. Arrange half the potatoes in a thick layer over the base of a deep ovenproof casserole. Cover with half the onions.

3 Arrange the chicken joints on top of the onions. Pour over any pan juices. Tuck the garlic cloves all around and scatter over the lemon rind. Sprinkle with the thyme and rosemary and tuck in the bay leaf. Season well with salt and pepper. Cover with the remaining onions and then the rest of the potatoes. Pour in the boiling stock, set over a moderate heat and bring slowly back to the boil.

4 Cut a circle of greaseproof paper (a 'cartouche') slightly larger than the diameter of the casserole dish, scrunch it up a bit and sit it on top of the potatoes to cover. Cover with a very tight-fitting lid (the dish should steam in its own juices) and bake for 1 hour.

5 Melt the remaining butter or fat, then uncover the potatoes and brush them with this. Return the casserole to the oven uncovered for about 20 minutes to allow the potatoes to brown. Serve with steamed young kale and glazed carrots.

# 93 Braised Chicken with Leeks, Bacon and Caramelized Onions

| |
|---|
| Informal supper |
| Preparation time 1¼ hours |
| Serves 4 |

**2 teaspoons chopped fresh thyme**

**4 x 175–200 g (6–7 oz) boneless chicken thighs, with skin left on**

**freshly ground sea salt and freshly ground black pepper**

**8 rashers of dry-cured streaky bacon, stretched with the back of a knife**

**50 g (2 oz) butter**

**3 large onions, thickly sliced**

**225 g (8 oz) leeks, split, washed and thickly sliced**

**1 garlic clove, crushed**

**2 teaspoons plain flour**

**300 ml (½ pint) passata**

**100 ml (3½ fl oz) Light Chicken Stock (see page 14)**

**new potatoes and buttered cabbage, to serve**

This is a recipe based on the onion-gravy idea of cooking onions until they are sweet and caramelized. In this version I include leeks and garlic. Leek skins vary in thickness, depending on their age, so if your leeks are very thick slice them more thinly so that they cook at the same rate as the onions. I love wrapping chicken thighs in bacon because they seem to merge into one – the saltiness contrasting so well with the sweet onions.

**1** Preheat the oven to 180°C/350°F/Gas Mark 4.

**2** Rub the thyme over the flesh side of the chicken thighs and season with salt and pepper. Reshape the thighs and then carefully roll 2 bacon rashers around each thigh.

**3** Melt the butter in a flameproof casserole and fry the chicken and bacon parcels until golden brown. Remove to a plate with a slotted spoon. Add the onions, cook for 5–6 minutes, then add the leeks and garlic to the casserole and cook for about 15 minutes, until everything has caramelized and turned a deep golden brown.

**4** Stir in the flour, mixing very well, and cook for 1 minute. Then add the passata and stock, stirring constantly, and bring to the boil. Season well and add the chicken and bacon parcels and any juices that may have collected. Cover and bake in the oven for 45 minutes until the chicken is tender.

**5** When the chicken is cooked, lift the parcels out of the casserole on to a warm serving dish, and then place the casserole over a medium heat and boil the liquid hard until it thickens. Adjust the seasoning if necessary, and pour the sauce over the chicken parcels. Serve with hot new potatoes and buttered cabbage.

# 94 Tagine of Chicken, Apricots and Mint

| |
|---|
| Informal supper |
| Preparation time 1 hour 5 minutes |
| Serves 4 |

50 g (2 oz) butter

6 x 140–175 g (5–6 oz) free-range or organic chicken thighs

1 onion, finely chopped

¼ teaspoon ground cumin

¼ teaspoon ground ginger

¼ teaspoon ground cinnamon

2 teaspoons sweet paprika

freshly ground sea salt and freshly ground black pepper

100 g (4 oz) ground almonds

juice and finely grated rind of 1 orange

600 ml (1 pint) Light Chicken Stock (see page 14)

175 g (6 oz) no-need-to-soak dried apricots

3 tablespoons chopped fresh mint, plus extra to garnish

couscous, to serve

A tagine is a Moroccan stew named after the closed dish in which it is cooked. It simmers for hours, concentrating the flavours and thickening the sauce. The whole dish, usually made out of terracotta, sits over glowing charcoal as it cooks. I've devised one using chicken thighs – free-range or organic ones will stand up to the long, slow cooking as the flesh is firmer than that of ordinary chickens. The ground almonds thicken the sauce and give it a really good flavour.

1 Preheat the oven to 160°C/325°F/Gas Mark 3. Melt the butter in the bottom of a large, heavy casserole. Brown the chicken thighs all over, three at a time, removing them to a plate as you go.

2 Stir the onion and spices into the juices at the bottom of the dish and cook for about 5 minutes to release the aroma and soften the onion a little. Season with salt and a good grinding of pepper. Stir in the ground almonds.

3 Return the chicken to the casserole with the orange juice and rind and cover with the stock. Bring to the boil and then turn the heat to very low. Cover the surface of the stew with a sheet of crumpled greaseproof paper (a 'cartouche') and then the lid – this will prevent too much steam escaping during the cooking. Bake in the oven for 30 minutes.

4 Add the apricots and mint, stir them into the liquid, and bake, uncovered, for a further 15 minutes. By this time the chicken should be falling off the bone and the apricots should be plump and the sauce thickened (if not, boil to reduce). Taste and adjust the seasoning, sprinkle with more mint and serve at the table with a big bowl of couscous.

# 95 Ratatouille Chicken

| Informal supper |
| --- |
| Preparation time 2 hours |
| Serves 4–6 |

**2 aubergines**

**freshly ground sea salt and freshly ground black pepper**

**4 x 140–175 g (5–6 oz) chicken thighs**

**4 chicken drumsticks**

**2 tablespoons white wine vinegar**

**3 teaspoons dried *herbes de Provence***

**3 peppers (any colour except green)**

**6 tablespoons olive oil**

**2 large onions, thinly sliced**

**2 garlic cloves, crushed**

**1 tablespoon finely crushed coriander seeds**

**5 tablespoons white wine**

**400 g can chopped tomatoes**

**1 teaspoon sugar**

**about 20 Greek-style black olives (the wrinkly ones)**

Ratatouille has an undeservedly naff image, stemming from its popularity at dinner parties in the 1970s. But it's a classic combination of Mediterranean flavours – aubergines, peppers, tomatoes and herbs. In my opinion, green peppers are not suitable – they are unripe, bitter and indigestible – so use any other colour of pepper for this. This is one of the occasions where using dried herbs is almost better than fresh. *Herbes de Provence* (basil, marjoram, thyme and rosemary) add that 'baked by the Mediterranean sun' flavour and crushed coriander seeds add an orangey, warm, earthy tone.

**1** Cut the aubergines into large bite-sized pieces, put them in a colander, sprinkle them well with salt and leave them to drain for 1 hour.

**2** Put the chicken thighs and drumsticks in a glass bowl, sprinkle with the vinegar and rub in the herbs. Cover and leave to marinate while the aubergines are losing their bitter juices.

**3** Preheat the oven to 190°C/375°F/Gas Mark 5. Halve the peppers, remove the white membrane and seeds and slice into thick strips. Heat half the olive oil in a flameproof casserole and fry the onions, garlic and coriander seeds until soft and transparent, but not coloured.

**4** Rinse and drain the aubergines and dry them on kitchen paper. Add the peppers and aubergines to the casserole and cook them for about 10 minutes, stirring occasionally until they are softening around the edges but not browning.

**5** In a frying pan, heat the remaining oil over a medium heat, and brown the chicken thighs and drumsticks all over, being careful not to get the pan too hot or the herbs will burn. Lay the chicken on top of the vegetables in the casserole. Now deglaze the frying pan with the wine, boiling to reduce it to a tablespoon, then add the tomatoes, sugar and olives. Pour this mixture over the chicken joints in the casserole, and give it a gentle push around with a wooden spoon to mix in the tomato. Bring to a simmer, season well and then cover with a lid and place in the oven for about 25 minutes or until the chicken is cooked.

# 96 Chicken with Root Vegetables and Barley

<table>
<tr><td>Low fat</td></tr>
<tr><td>Preparation time 40 minutes</td></tr>
<tr><td>Serves 4</td></tr>
</table>

1 onion

2 carrots

2 celery sticks

2 leeks, split and washed

2 parsnips, peeled

175 g (6 oz) swede (neep), peeled

2 large potatoes, peeled

25 g (1 oz) butter

3 tablespoons olive oil

8 chicken pieces (4 drumsticks and 4 thighs)

40 g (1½ oz) pearl barley

2 teaspoons tomato purée

1 tablespoon plain flour

600 ml (1 pint) Light Chicken Stock (see page 14)

freshly ground sea salt and freshly ground black pepper

2 tablespoons chopped fresh tarragon

This is Scotch broth in disguise. Being a Scot I love the combination of barley and root vegetables. They have an earthy richness so suited to chicken. At home we grow a fine selection of root vegetables and this is a good way to incorporate them into a one-pot dish. On a cold winter's day this dish feels as though it does you good.

**1** Cut all the vegetables into large chunks. Heat the butter and olive oil in a large non-stick frying pan and, when the butter is foaming, add the chicken joints. Carefully brown all over and transfer to a flameproof casserole.

**2** Add the vegetables to the frying pan and fry over a high heat until well browned. Add the pearl barley and tomato purée and cook for 2–3 minutes. Stir in the flour and then gradually stir in the stock. Pour over the chicken and vegetables, set the casserole dish over the heat and season to taste with salt and pepper. Cover and simmer gently for 25 minutes. When the cooking time is up, check that the chicken and vegetables are tender; if not, give them a few more minutes.

**3** Stir in the tarragon and simmer for 1 minute. Check the seasoning, then serve.

# 97 Spanish Chicken with Capers and Prunes

| |
|---|
| Informal supper |
| Preparation time 35 minutes, plus marinating time |
| Serves 4 |

**4 boneless chicken breasts, with skin left on**

**1 tablespoon sunflower oil**

**2 tablespoons light brown sugar**

**6 tablespoons dry white wine**

**1 bay leaf**

**1 tablespoon chopped fresh flatleaf parsley**

**new potatoes, to serve**

**FOR THE MARINADE:**

**4 tablespoons olive oil**

**4 teaspoons red wine vinegar**

**2 garlic cloves, crushed**

**1 tablespoon salted capers, rinsed**

**16 green olives, stoned**

**8 prunes, stoned and halved**

**1 teaspoon freeze-dried oregano**

**freshly ground sea salt and freshly ground black pepper**

John Webber cooked this Spanish dish for my wife Holly and me when we returned from a summer holiday – after tasting it we felt as if we had never left the sunshine, so it had to go in the book. The contrast of sweet prunes and salty pungent capers and olives gives this a very Mediterranean flavour. It is really good served hot and almost better served cold with a plain potato salad.

**1** Start the day before. Take the chicken breasts and make two or three slashes through the skin, cutting a little way into the flesh. Then make the marinade by mixing all the ingredients in a bowl. Lay the breasts in a shallow glass or stainless steel dish and spoon over the marinade, rubbing it into the cuts. Place the covered dish in the fridge and leave overnight.

**2** The next day, preheat the oven to 190°C/375°F/Gas Mark 5. Lift the chicken breasts from the marinade and drain well, keeping the marinade. Heat the sunflower oil in a flameproof casserole that will take the breasts in a single layer. Fry the breasts, skin-sides down, until the skins are a light golden brown. Turn the breasts over and remove the casserole from the heat to cool a little.

**3** Pour the reserved marinade over the breasts and then sprinkle on the brown sugar. Pour the wine around the chicken breasts and tuck in the bay leaf. Cover with a lid and place in the oven for about 20 minutes, basting the chicken occasionally (cook a little longer if the breasts are very thick). Pierce the thickest part of a breast with a skewer and check the juices are running clear with no trace of blood.

**4** Lift the breasts on to a serving dish and return the casserole to the heat. Bring the juices to a simmer and add the parsley. Mix well and check the seasoning, then pour the contents of the casserole over the hot chicken. Serve with plain boiled new potatoes.

# 98 Chicken with Chorizo, Red Peppers and Butter Beans

| Informal supper |
| --- |
| Preparation time 55 minutes |
| Serves 4 |

1 tablespoon olive oil

8 chicken pieces (4 drumsticks and 4 thighs)

175 g (6 oz) fresh Spanish chorizo sausage, cubed

1 onion, finely diced

2 large garlic cloves, crushed

1 teaspoon mild chilli powder (see page 92)

3 red Romano peppers, halved, seeded and cut into chunks

400 g (14 oz) passata

2 tablespoons tomato purée

150 ml (¼ pint) chicken stock (a cube will do)

400 g can butter beans plus a 200 g can butter beans, drained

a small bunch of fresh thyme

1 bay leaf

freshly ground sea salt and freshly ground black pepper

200 g bag of baby spinach leaves

3 tablespoons roughly chopped fresh coriander or parsley

I often use the combination of soft butter beans, the oily paprika flavour from the chorizo and soft red peppers in soups and stews, but it really is best with chicken pieces. Use the thin-skinned long Romano peppers, which really melt into the sauce while the oil and paprika soak into the beans. To incorporate a green vegetable into this, I stir in spinach to wilt into the stew – you could use red chard, pak choi or even mustard leaves instead.

1 Preheat the oven to 190°C/375°F/Gas Mark 5. Heat the olive oil in a heavy flameproof casserole and brown the chicken pieces all over. Lift them out on to a plate and add the chorizo to the casserole. Cook the chorizo for 2–3 minutes until the red oil starts to run and then add the onion, garlic and mild chilli powder and cook over a low heat for about 5 minutes, until soft.

2 Now add the peppers and cook for another 2–3 minutes to soften them. Stir in the passata, tomato purée, stock, beans, thyme and bay leaf. Cover and simmer for 10 minutes. Season to taste with salt and pepper.

3 Return the chicken pieces and any juices to the casserole, bring to a simmer, then cover and bake in the oven for about 25 minutes. Remove from the oven and uncover. (If the sauce looks too watery, place the casserole over a medium heat and boil to reduce until nice and thick.) Stir in the spinach and coriander or parsley. Allow the spinach to wilt into the stew. Remove the thyme and bay leaf from the casserole, then serve.

# 99 Quick Chicken Cassoulet

| Smart entertaining |
| --- |
| Preparation time 1 hour |
| Serves 5 |

2 tablespoons olive oil

2 x 130 g packets of lardons (*cubetti di pancetta*)

1 large onion, sliced

3–4 large garlic cloves, chopped

6 x 140–175 g (5–6 oz) chicken thighs

6 Toulouse or chunky Italian sausages

3 x 400 g cans of butterbeans, drained and rinsed

about 300 ml (½ pint) Light Chicken Stock (page 14, or a chicken stock cube will do)

2 tablespoons tomato purée

400 g can chopped tomatoes

2 bay leaves

1 teaspoon dried thyme

75 g (3 oz) stale white bread-crumbs

freshly ground sea salt and freshly ground black pepper

A real cassoulet can take days to make, soaking beans and adding everything really slowly, but who has the time? This recipe has all the fantastic flavour combinations of bacon, chicken, garlic, beans and sausage but by using creamy canned butter beans the whole process is speeded up. It would raise the hackles on any French chef's back, but making classic recipes achievable within today's time constraints is the *raison d'être* of this book!

**1** Preheat the oven to 190°C/375°F/Gas Mark 5.

**2** Heat 1 tablespoon of the oil in a non-stick frying pan and brown the bacon. Tip into a shallow flameproof casserole (which has a lid) and then add the onion and garlic to the frying pan and fry for 5 minutes, until softening. Tip them into the casserole.

**3** Reheat the frying pan, add the other tablespoon of oil and fry the chicken thighs until golden brown all over. Lift these into the casserole and then fry the sausages and add to the casserole. Pour the beans over the chicken and sausages. Deglaze the frying pan with the stock, adding the tomato purée, canned tomatoes and herbs. Stir well, then pour over the beans. Give it a gentle stir and bring to the boil on top of the stove. Season to taste with salt and pepper.

**4** Remove from the heat and sprinkle the breadcrumbs over the surface in a thick, even layer. Bake in the oven for about 30 minutes until a golden crust is formed. Serve warm.

# 100  Chicken Legs Braised in Olive Oil

| Informal supper |
| :--- |
| Preparation time 3½ hours, plus chilling time |
| Serves 4 |

**4 chicken legs (thighs and drumsticks joined)**

**4 tablespoons fine sea salt**

**3 garlic cloves, roughly sliced**

**a couple of sprigs of fresh thyme**

**a couple of bay leaves**

**at least 600 ml (1 pint) olive oil**

**2 tablespoons light soy sauce (preferably Japanese)**

**4 tablespoons runny honey**

**15 g (½ oz) butter**

**750 g (1½ lb) cabbage or spring greens, shredded**

**½ teaspoon ground cumin**

**freshly ground sea salt and freshly ground black pepper**

This recipe is based on the old French technique of confit, traditionally used to cook and preserve ducks' legs in duck fat. This is a more modern and healthier version using chicken legs and olive oil, but still splendidly tasty. The chicken legs are salted to draw out excess moisture, then stewed for ages in olive oil flavoured with herbs. They are then crisped in the oven, which releases more fat, and the result is golden, crisp legs with tender, flavoursome meat.

**1** The day before, prepare the chicken. Lay the chicken legs in a glass or stainless steel dish and rub the salt all over them. Turn the legs skin-sides up. Tuck the garlic, thyme and bay leaves amongst and under the legs. Cover with cling film and pop in the fridge overnight.

**2** The next day, preheat the oven to 160°C/325°F/Gas Mark 3 if you're going to cook the legs in the oven. Heat the olive oil in a casserole dish over a low heat. Meanwhile, take the chicken legs from the fridge, rub off the excess salt and rinse under running water. Pat the legs dry, taking care to remove as much moisture as possible – you don't want a mass of hissing when you add the legs to oil! Pick out the garlic and herbs, rinse and pat dry. Once the oil is warm, lower the legs into the oil and add the rinsed and dried herbs and garlic for flavour. Making sure the legs are covered by the oil, put on the lid and cook very slowly either on top of the stove or in the preheated oven for 3 hours. They can then be refrigerated, covered by the oil, until needed.

**3** To finish the legs, preheat the oven to 220°C/425°F/Gas Mark 7. Lift the legs from the casserole, pat dry and lay them on a rack set over a roasting tin. Mix together the soy sauce and honey and use to baste the chicken. Roast at the top of the oven for 10–15 minutes, turning once or twice until the skin is crisp and golden.

**4** Whilst roasting the legs, melt the butter in a frying pan and sauté the cabbage or spring greens until softened, but not coloured. Stir in the cumin and season with salt and pepper.

**5** To serve, place a generous portion of greens in the centre of each plate and top with a chicken leg. Bring the remaining soy sauce and honey mixture to the boil and drizzle over or around the chicken.

# Index

## Food photography by Philip Webb

Published by BBC Books, BBC Worldwide Ltd,
80 Wood Lane, London W12 0TT

First published 2004
© Nick Nairn 2004
The moral right of the author has been asserted.

Food photography © BBC Worldwide
(pages 8 and 9 by Stephen Kearney)

All rights reserved. No part of this book may
be reproduced in any form or by any means,
without permission in writing from the publisher,
except by a reviewer who may quote brief
passages in a review.

ISBN 0 563 48704 6

Commissioning Editor: Nicky Ross
Project Editor: Sarah Miles
Copy-editor: Deborah Savage
Cover Art Director: Pene Parker
Book Designer/Photo Art Director: Lisa Pettibone
Home Economist: Maxine Clark
Stylist: Helen Trent
Production Controller: Arlene Alexander

Set in Caecilia and Foundry Sans
Printed and bound in Singapore by Tien Wah Press
Colour separations by Radstock Reproductions Ltd,
Midsomer Norton

If you require further information on any BBC
Worldwide product call 08700 777 001 or visit
our website on www.bbcshop.com

Many thanks to Nicky Ross at BBC Books for the
concept of the Top 100 series and for sticking
with it, also to Sarah Miles, Pene Parker and Lisa
Pettibone for creating such a good-looking book.
Special thanks to Maxine Clark for inspiration,
recipe testing and food styling (I really don't
think I could have done this without her!), and
to my assistant, Nadine Carmichael, for the
considerable time, effort and good humour she
put into this book. A big thank you to Philip
Webb for more wonderful photographs and last,
but not least, to John Webber and his team at
Nairns Cook School for their ongoing support.